To the memory of Martha Jane Cox,
my beloved "Nanny," who at the
age of 99 was still proclaiming the
victory of the Lord.

"For our struggle is not against flesh and blood, but against the powers of this dark world and against the spiritual forces of evil in the heavenly realms."

Ephesians 6:12 (NIV)

Do you sometimes feel you are fighting an uphill battle in spiritual matters? Are you trying to persevere with faith in a particular area of your life? In *The Weapons of Our Warfare,* Coleman and Mary Phillips explain the types of combat believers face constantly and equip you for victory. In this clear, biblical discussion, they give evidence of the reality of the powers of darkness in the world today. They alert you to many guises Satan uses to defeat believers and thwart God's purposes. Most important, the authors show how to use the weapons that prevail over Satan, including the blood of Jesus, fasting, and praise and worship. Here is an effective strategy for gaining a stronghold against the forces of evil; you will find yourself winning new ground for Jesus Christ. Your entire walk in the Lord will be strengthened as you see the working power of the weapons God has given us for spiritual warfare.

T H E
WEAPONS
O F   O U R
WARFARE

P.O. Box 462806
Escondido, CA
92046-2806

Written by
Coleman Phillips
with Mary Phillips

Foreword by
Jack Hayford

CONTENTS

Foreword

Coleman Phillips has touched a nerve! You're about to be stirred, taught, shaken, blessed, and heartwarmed. In these pages you will not only meet the truth, but you'll experience its power to ignite action. You can't read this and be the same.

It is an inescapable fact that the majority of Christ's sincerest followers are without understanding of the spiritual arena, its dimensions, its warfare, its resources, and its practical meaning to us all. But, to my opinion, it is equally inescapable that this book provides a solid, balanced, efficiently concise answer to our need for insight in that realm.

I love the here-and-now practicality of this book. In perusing these pages I have been refreshed and reminded; had my spirit invigorated and inspired anew, as well as had my mind sharpened to a keener edge for the struggle against hell's dark powers.

Foreword

I want you to prepare for an adventure not in the glib superficial sense of the word, but in the classic sense of moving forward and outward into realms of discovery that too few have found. The summons today is to discernment and dynamic–to seeing the real warfare to be fought, and to being equipped to fight it. *Weapons of our Warfare* shows the way and gives the tools. Here is a handbook for developing an essential facet of the believer's life; a handbook that ought to become a text resource for adult studies in every prospective leader.

One last thing.

I'm thankful I've been a friend of Coleman and Mary Phillips since the days Anna and I were with them at study on the same college campus. With the passage of years I've watched this man and woman rise as pillars of strength as models of fruitfulness and fidelity to Christ. Coleman is a gifted scholar, a powerful communicator, a faithful pastor, an exciting teacher, and a true gentleman. Mary, who so ably assists him in this book as she does in their ministry, is the complete feminine counterpart to each of those qualities I've ascribed to him.

It's an honor to be asked to introduce their work to you. But not as great an honor as to be friends of theirs, as well as partners and fellow-soldiers with them in last-days' spiritual warfare.

Jack W. Hayford

The Church on the Way
Van Nuys, California

1
The Call

Put on the whole armour of God, that ye may be able to stand against the wiles of the devil.

Ephesians 6:11, KJV

I had been in the ministry for fifteen years when I suffered what was diagnosed initially as a heart attack. Three weeks of hospitalization and hours of testing revealed that I had in fact collapsed from exhaustion. My strength was at an end—and so, it seemed, was my ministry.

During those months of weakness I often agonized before the Lord, not only for healing, but for instruction and direction. At a point of deep despair, the Lord reminded me of an event that happened in the early days of my Christian experience.

The Weapons of our Warfare

While attending college in Los Angeles, I rode the Olympic Boulevard late-night bus to my home in Beverly Hills. Usually I was the lone passenger.

On night as I bumped sleepily along, I was suddenly riveted to my seat by an incredible stillness. I don't know that the voice was audible, but it was unmistakably the Father's:

> *Son, I am drawing a line down the middle of My Church. On one side will be all those who are for the Holy Spirit. On the other side will be all those who resist His work.*

I was such a new Christian and so ignorant of the work of the Holy Spirit or the workings of the church in general that I thought something that equaled, "Oh, really, Lord!" I tucked the incident away as just another gentle visit of His presence.

Not long after, I was in my living room praying. The Holy Spirit virtually commanded me to pick up pen and paper. As He spoke to me, I wrote in part:

> *I have not called you to be other than a vessel for My glory. There need be no man glorified in any ministry. Hold up the Son and all men will come to the fount for drink. If men come to the fount, their thirst will be met through the Son, but if man comes to another man, his thirst shall not be quenched. Hearken to the Spirit, magnify His name, and your works will prosper and a great harvest will be gathered.*

12

The Call

At the time I was so naïve spiritually that I could not begin to interpret all the things that were said to me. I typed it out and would occasionally ponder the message. Obviously it confirmed my call to ministry and that seemed enough at the time.

During the years that followed I would ask persons I respected why there were so few gifts of the Spirit in operation in the Church. Sometimes my questions were evaded. Sometimes they were answered simply, "I don't know."

The feeling expressed most often was that which my wife, Mary, who had gone through what was commonly known as the "Latter Rain Movement" of the '40s, advised: "Be careful. You don't want to get into fanaticism."

As I recuperated from my illness, the Lord was bringing those early words back to my memory. What was going on? Was my collapse His way to get my attention? If so, I needed to listen, to regroup, to prepare for what He wanted me to do. Whatever it was, or wherever it was, I made up my mind that my next venture into ministry would give precedence to the patterns that were laid down by the Holy Spirit in the early Church.

Some months later a call came to pastor a small congregation in Hillsboro, Oregon. It was there I would learn about spiritual warfare. It was there I would learn how to recognize the real enemy. It was there I would learn about my spiritual arsenal.

As in most churches, there was a core of faithful people who had kept the church viable through the years. It soon became apparent, however, that the people were not nearly as enthusiastic about functioning in New Testament patterns as was their pastor. Folks of good intentions, they simply were not anxious to change.

It turned into a do or die situation for me. Either God's plan would work or I would leave the ministry. I had no idea how to go about making it work, and as months passed Mary and I felt as though we were in a losing battle with them. Little did we know we were battling on the wrong front!

It was during this time that our supervisor for the Foursquare Churches came to our rescue. He explained that God had provided weapons that guaranteed we would always be victors and not victims. Through his guidance we began to identify and deal with our true enemy–not the members of our congregation, but Satan himself!

You see, most of my ministry and much of my Christian life had been spent reacting to people. It took me fifteen years to discover that my fight was not against flesh and blood. Before this discovery when something mean and nasty happened–some brother or sister would tell me they didn't like the way I looked or preached or whatever–I felt that person was my enemy and I needed to get in there and straighten him out. The same thing was true of friendships–and even in the home and on the job.

Finally I realized that this is one of the enemy's greatest deceptions: If Satan can get us fighting against each other, he knows we will lose. While we are grappling with the wrong enemy, the real one goes unchallenged and wins by default.

The Call

All the time that we were trying to change the people in our church we should have been coming "against principalities, against powers, against the rulers of the darkness of this world, against spiritual wickedness in high places" (Ephesians 6:12 KJV) that were blocking our forward move in the Spirit.

But just how does one grapple with these nebulous creatures? They can't be confronted with evidence of their crimes. They can't be dismissed from church membership.

It was as though we had been introduced to a vast arsenal of potent weaponry. As we explored our powerful resources, it became evident that we had opened a heavenly armory that had a specialized weapon designed to defeat every enemy. And it was not available to preachers only! It was open to everyone.

2
The Fact of Spiritual Warfare

Let us go up at once, and possess [the land]; for we are well able to overcome it.
Numbers 13:30, KJV

After I taught on spiritual warfare one Sunday morning, Stuart Barnes*, a man in my congregation, came to me following the morning service.

"I don't agree with you at all," he said. "In fact I think what you are teaching is dangerous. I don't want to stir the devil up. If I leave him alone, he'll leave me alone. If I go after him, he might come after me!"

Mr. Barnes is not alone in his resistance to this message.

---

*Not his real name.

17

The Weapons of our Warfare

Many Christians consider spiritual warfare to be a negative subject. Of course, if all I did was preach on spiritual warfare, if I didn't balance this subject with the ringing affirmations of the Gospel of Jesus Christ, then the criticism would be justified. But the Gospel message is about both good and evil, joy and sorrow, death and resurrection. It is very much about the enemy of believers - and how we can triumph over him.

Therefore, it is to Stuart Barnes - and all believers like him, who have doubts or questions or fears or plain resistance to the idea of spiritual warfare - that this book is addressed.

Two men in our present church collaborated on a book for children which would teach mature Biblical concepts including the importance of battling Satan and his minions. One is an authority in early childhood education. The other is a talented illustrator. Both have published prior works. The book is beautiful in its production and excellent in its content.

All the publishing houses they sent it to responded favorably but all turned the book down. "We don't dare publish this because the concept of spiritual warfare is too controversial," one admitted.

Controversial with whom? Denominations? Ministers? Certain people? In reality these individuals and groups have succumbed to the strategy of the enemy.

Satan loves our reluctance to credit him with evil and to learn to fight him. He stands in our midst and thinks, "Ah, this will be an easy victory. No one suspects I'm at work." And all the time he is carrying out his campaign - mostly undetected. Why does Ephesians 6 exhort us to put on the whole armor of God if we are not headed for battle?

When things go wrong in the lives of some Christians, they mistakenly conclude that it is God who is out to get them. They blame Him and become bitter against Him.

The Scriptures teach there is one who is for us and one who is against us. "What shall we say then? If God be for us, who can be against us?" (Rom. 8:31). A clearer translation here is, "Who can be against us successfully?"

As believers, we must acknowledge that there IS a spiritual realm which is far more real than the natural realm around us that we can see and understand. Just as we accept by faith the reality of God, we must also accept by faith the truth that we have an enemy who is not visible to the physical eye.

Revelation 12:4 states that one-third of the angelic host fell in rebellion with Lucifer and was consequently expelled from heaven. It seems reasonable to believe, in the total view of Scripture, that these are the powerful beings Paul designates as our enemy in Ephesians 6.

If a believer retreats from confrontation with his enemy, a gradual erosion of dynamic spiritual life begins. Under the cloak of anonymity, Satan is able to drain out the power and vitality of Jesus operating in that life. Whether we want to acknowledge it or not - and the basic premise of this book is that - we are always in warfare with the devil.

Once we have been convinced that, like it or not, we are doing battle with principalities, powers, rulers of darkness of the world, and spiritual wickedness in high places, a second, happier awareness comes. We are not asked to win the war. We are only asked to do mopping up operations. Victory has already been declared! Jesus, long ago, triumphed over the enemy.

> *And you, being dead in your trespasses and the uncircumcision of your flesh, He has made alive together with Him, having forgiven you all trespasses, having wiped out the handwriting of requirements that was against us,which was contrary to us. And He has taken it out of the way, having nailed it to the cross.* Having disarmed principalities and powers, *He made a public spectacle of them, triumphing over them in it.*
> Colossians 2:13-15 NKJ

During World War II I was attached to the 9th Armored Division going into Germany. On May 8, 1945, V.E. Day, victory was declared in Europe. The war was over. Everybody said so. The announcement came directly from Eisenhower's command. We were now supposed to be an army of occupation, yet three days after V.E. Day I had my boot buckle shot off by a sniper! There were still pockets of resistance that had not surrendered. The land was not ours until we occupied it. Until we did so, our safety was precarious.

Israel had much the same experience. As recorded in Numbers 13:2 the Lord said, "I have given you the land." A gift - flat out! Unconditionally! Well, with a bit of a condition, "Now go in and take it."

You know what happened. Joshua and Caleb saw the land flowing with milk and honey. They brought back the good grapes of Eschol.

But the other scouts said, "There are giants in the land. We can't stand up against the forces of darkness and the intimidation of such a powerful enemy."

That paraphrase is mine; but this phrase is theirs, "We are as grasshoppers in our own sight."

Instead of seeing themselves as people whom the God of this universe had commissioned and actually told, "Go in. Take it. I give it to you," they let fear destroy their self-perception. Instead of seeing themselves as the victorious host of the Lord, they saw themselves as helpless as grasshoppers.

Their unbelief was a sore point with the Lord. Hebrews 3:4 tells us: "Because of UNBELIEF, they could not enter in."

We are living in an era when all believers are being challenged with new crises, new appropriations of alien territory, new giants to overcome and new opportunities to enter in! We can either pass over and see the giants fall, or be passed by and spend the rest of our lives in the bleak barrenness of a spiritual desert.

In the fourteenth chapter of Numbers, the sinful Israelites who had murmured against the Lord tried finally to get it together. But the opportunity for victorious conquest had passed them by. They were never allowed to enjoy the land

God had promised. Their bones were left to bleach in the desert.

But it is not too late for us. Everyone of us stands at a borderline of faith. Either we will be frightened away by the prospect of battle or in the spirit of Joshua and Caleb we will say, "The Lord said we could have the good things of the land if we would take them. We are well able to do it. Let's go for it— now!"

3
Scouting the Enemy's Camp

Your adversary the devil prowls around like a roaring lion, seeking some one to devour. 1 Peter 5:8, RSV

Probably the all-time depressing incident in my ministerial preparation days was a visit to a historic church led by an equally historic pastor. If your mind is picturing "museum," you are on the right track. As a senior student, I had been asked to bring the evening message.

When we met in the anteroom, the pastor laid a gentle hand on my shoulder. "Son, don't be discouraged with the small crowd tonight. I've done everything I know to get these people away from swimming pools and barbecues on Sunday evening, but nothing works."

My heart went out to him. He had been a powerful preacher in past years. Now, in his evening of full-time ministry, he was weary and disheartened.

"What do you think the problem is?" I asked.

"Well, my boy, I believe we are in the great falling away. Jesus is coming soon. I'm just trying to hold on and be faithful to the end."

My heart sank. The thought of spending the productive years of my ministerial life holding on during a great falling away did not fill me with excitement.

"If this is the extent of ministry, Lord," I thought, *"I hope You return fast!"*

What this blessed brother had lost sight of was the manipulation of the people in his church by the enemy of their souls. The pleasures of California living had been the bait the enemy used to lure them away. Sitting sadly by would not release them. It would take a powerful blow of a spiritual weapon to smash this stronghold.

Look at this Scripture:

> *Jesus answered and said to him, Blessed are you Simon Bar-jonah, for flesh and blood has not revealed this to you, but my Father who is in heaven. And I also say to you that you are Peter, and on this rock, I will build My church, and the gates of hell shall not prevail against it.*
>
> Matthew 16:17,18 NKJ

Scouting the Enemy's Camp

Perhaps it was a traditional interpretation or maybe it was my own misguided explication, but before I understood spiritual warfare, this passage always meant this to me:

True, we are in a battle with Satan. And true, Jesus has won the victory - ultimately. But in the meantime, we are fighting a war of containment, sort of a spiritual Vietnam. There will be enclaves where we are in control, but for the most part we are not to pursue the enemy aggressively. We are certainly not to invade *his* kingdom. We are just to stand at the gates of Hell and snatch as many passersby as possible from eternal destruction.

It was Jack Hayford, pastor of The Church on the Way in Van Nuys, California, who first called my attention to the fact that gates represented authority. For instance, persons in authority in ancient Middle Eastern cities would meet at the gates to administer government. This came as a powerful revelation to me. This verse really meant that I was seated in the gate of authority and my decisions overruled the decisions of Hell!

Notice, it is not the keys *to* the kingdom, but keys *of* the kingdom that are given to us. That means Satan can't landlock us anywhere. We have been given divine easement and access to every part of the Kingdom of God.

It is easy to hold such beliefs in theory; you can be certain Satan will always challenge the tenacity with which we are willing to implement them: "Who do *you* think you are? What are you doing in my territory? Don't you know you are on dangerous ground? What do you think you can do against me?"

25

The Weapons of our Warfare

Now it is true that Jesus said that Satan has a kingdom: *And if Satan cast out Satan, he is divided against himself. How then shall HIS kingdom stand?*

Matthew 12:25b NKJ

And Satan is described as having authority:

Again the devil taketh him up into an exceedingly high mountain and showed him all the kingdoms of the world, and their glory and said to him, "All these things I will give You if You will fall down and worship me.

Matthew 4:8,9 NKJ

Jesus did not argue the prerogative that Satan was claiming during this time of temptation. He didn't say, "These things are not yours to offer." In fact, in this same context, Jesus refers to Satan as the god of this world. Some scholars even believe that this planet at one time may have been the actual realm of Satan and the seat of his authority.

Whatever claim Satan has held on this planet in the past, we know for certain God has chosen this earth as the arena in which Satan will be defeated. Satan used man to bring about the fall of God's lovely creation - and God has planned that the redemption of that creation will come through the Son of Man, Jesus Christ.

This is at the heart of all spiritual warfare. Satan is rallying his evil troops to keep humanity from redemption. Jesus has called and equipped his followers to do battle against him.

26

Frightening as that may seem to an inexperienced believer, the outcome is fixed. We have weapons that are mighty to the tearing down of Satan's strongholds (2 Corinthians 10:4).

God's strategy has never been to fight a defensive war of containment against Satan's attacks. His plan has always been to move in offensive battle - pushing out the boundaries of the Kingdom of God, crushing the resistance of the enemy, moving into places where he has been in command, pulling down every stronghold where he has been ensconced. The authority - the gates - of hell is not going to be able to stop us, let alone defeat us.

Timidly, I myself began to walk past those forbidden gates. As I began to scout out the enemy's camp. His profile became familiar to me.

He *is* strong. He *is* malicious - and he is an expert in staging attack. He's been at it a long time, and he keeps books on each Christian. Vulnerable areas are circled in red and coded for instant thrust. He is invisible and a master of disguise. He plays by no set of ethical rules. He attacks wherever, whomever, whenever he can. He originated hit-and-run.

And he is well-organized. Ephesians 6 spells out the structure of his forces. There are principalities devoted to geographical activities. There are powers that infiltrate and energize the governing forces of the universe. There are rulers of the darkness of this world who keep the imps and demons at their proper assignations. There is spiritual wickedness in high places that endeavors to systematize error and produce such a perfect counterfeit of truth that only those willing to receive God's truth are able to detect it.

The Weapons of our Warfare

Regional forces exhibit themselves in a number of ways. Certain crimes may be prevalent in a community. There may be a high incidence of family problems - divorce, abuse, incest, etc. There may be a hardness toward spiritual things and all churches find it difficult to accomplish their mission. On the other hand, certain types of religions and cults may flourish. Personal oppression results as individuals begin to live with fear, mistrust, anxiety and all the other phobias of modern life.

My first forays into the enemy's territory were both exhilarating and frightening. They were exhilarating because I discovered that the enemy —no matter what chilling form he took—always fled when I lifted my weapons. There were other times when, like the servant of Elisha, I felt as if I were surrounded by the horses and chariots of the enemy, as if I were alone on alien territory. Then as with the servant, the Lord opened my eyes and I saw that the mountain was full of His horses and chariots of fire - and those who were with me were more than those who were with the enemy (2 Kings 6:16,17).

It was only a temporary pastoral assignment. I knew beforehand that the church was in deep moral and financial trouble. My instructions were to "clean the place up" and return to my previous post. We soon discovered the church was merely a microcosm of the community. The local newspaper read like a scandal sheet. "Cleaning up" would be no easy task.

Scouting the Enemy's Camp

"How in the world do you minister in this sanctuary?" the old visiting missionary asked. "Don't you know the place is filled with mocking spirits?"

I knew something was wrong. Every sermon ended up in the rafters. There was no response on the part of the congregation. The sinning members were defiant and the others were discouraged. Nothing we did seemed to heal the wounds. But evil spirits in the sanctuary? I honestly thought the old fellow had been in the jungles too long.

"What you need to do," he continued, "is to walk through the building with your wife. Anoint the seats with oil and in the name of Jesus command those mocking spirits to leave the house of the Lord."

"What have we got to lose?" my wife said, and we began our own cleansing of the temple. There was no dramatic scene to be forever emblazoned on our memories, but the next Sunday morning, two people received Jesus as Savior. The church began to grow again. Finances improved. Broken relationships were mended. Feuding stopped. The pastor who was permanently assigned stayed for a number of years and the congregation became influential in bringing social and civic order back into the community.

Recognizing hell's regional forces and entering into combat with them is a difficult concept for some people, but I am convinced we are not going to succeed as we should if we do not come to grips with this principle.

An amazing encounter is recorded in Daniel between a messenger of the Lord, and the Prince of Persia:

The Weapons of our Warfare

Do not fear, Daniel, for from the first day that you set your heart to understand, and to humble yourself before your God, your words were heard; and I have come because of your words, but the prince of the kingdom of Persia withstood me twenty-one days, and behold, Michael one of the chief princes, came to help me, for I had been left alone with the kings of Persia.　　　　Daniel 10:12 NKJ

Naturally, everyone is free to have his own understanding of this passage and even to reject the whole idea of Satan's regional forces, but I speak from experience when I say that in our ministry I have not only encountered, but I have wrestled with and seen such forces defeated.

A number of years ago while we were in our motel room awaiting our first interview with the church council as to whether or not we would take our present pastorate in Escondido, California, we prayed and asked the Lord what we were coming into in the spiritual arena if we accepted this church.

Religious confusion was the term that immediately came to our spirits. We knew nothing of the history of churches in Escondido. We knew the church we were taking was one of good report, and this word did not have meaning in the immediate context.

It did not take long for us to understand that Satan's stronghold was indeed religious confusion. The geographic area has been a haven for the occult and cults. The historic churches have split - and resplit. The evangelical churches are no better off. And the Charismatics - their divisions were of national notoriety. A grim joke here was that store-front rentals were the hottest property in Escondido. Let one sit vacant a week and someone would start a church in it.

There is a spiritual wantonness in the Christian community that keeps people wandering from one ministry to another. If nothing available satisfies, they start something new. When the newness wears off, they move on. Submission, commitment, involvement are not significant characteristics other than when they are connected with self-gratification.

As we accepted the call to the church and stood against religious confusion using weapons from our spiritual arsenal, a word from the Lord came to us through a young man in our congregation. "I believe," he said, "God wants us to build an incredibly credible church here."

The Sunday morning services at first averaged between 125 and 150. Within five years Sunday morning attendance had passed the 1,000 mark. Finances in every department were growing. A new sanctuary was erected, expansion properties acquired.

Out of this church ministries have thrust themselves into the community and the world. In addition to the vision for Christian education at the elementary school level which the church has long fulfilled, a fine Bible College is now graduating ministers. Strong churches are being established in nearby communities. Ministers are being sent to other countries.

The Weapons of our Warfare

We clearly see our task as dispelling the forces of confusion by laying down strong and permanent foundations for the household of faith. There are still wanderers in the maze of confusion, but we have seen the forces of darkness yield as we wage progressive warfare against them. We will continue to work at becoming "incredible." In the meantime, those principalities are giving way to a solid, credible congregation of believers.

Besides becoming familiar with the personality of our enemy and the structure of his kingdom, once one presses beyond the gates of hell he soon gets the lay of the land on which the battle takes place.

Dr. Paul Bilheimer describes this well in his book, *Destined for the Throne,* when he cites the battle of the Amalakites with Israel (Exodus 17:8). To an observer, the battlefield was in the valley. That's where the flesh and blood soldiers were assembled. On looking closer, however, one would have noted that when the man sitting far up on the mountainside raised his arm, the battle went to the Israelites. If it came down, the Amalakites prevailed.

Where would you say the real action was? In the valley with the soldiers or on the mountain with Moses? A common ruse of the enemy is to confuse us in the heat of battle as to where the zone of combat is really located.

Satan introduces ideas into the thought patterns of individuals to try and stir up a bitter confrontation. When we raise the rod of the Spirit, it is amazing to see his forces shrink and truth and love conquer in the name of Jesus.

32

Scouting the Enemy's Camp

Jesus ran into the same satanic ruse. He had just announced the fact to His disciples that He was going to die. Peter, one of his chosen disciples responded, "Let it be far from You, Lord!"

With divine discernment Jesus quickly responded, "Get thee behind Me, Satan, for thou savorest not the things of God." He recognized that the apostle's words were not motivated by faith, but suggested by the enemy to prevent Peter from understanding the redemptive work that Jesus was about to undertake.

We must realize as we explore the enemy's territory that he does not own any of the land. He is merely a squatter, a usurper, a pretender. When you reestablish the claim of the Kingdom of God, he has no legal recourse. He must flee! Now that we've scouted the enemy's camp, it's time to take inventory of the homeland.

4
Commissioned by the King

"Behold, I give you the authority . . . over all the power of the enemy."   Luke 10:19, NKJ

Once one begins to understand the structure of the Kingdom of Darkness, the spiritual warrior needs to become thoroughly familiar with the operation of the Kingdom of God.

My understanding of the Kingdom of God was severely limited by my strong adherence to the dispensational approach to the Scriptures. This is the interpretation of Scriptures that divides God's working with His people into historic segments. One of the better known interpreters who used this approach was C. I. Scofield of Scofield Bible fame.

Dr. Scofield's notes were so valuable to me in my early Bible studies that I gave them more weight than even Dr. Scofield would have desired.

A few sentences cannot adequately describe this interpretive view which has wide acceptance among conservative churches. Basically, it says the theme of the Kingdom of God is not relevant during the time we live which they designate as the church age. They believe that the Kingdom of God and its authority will be the structure that God will use during the 1,000 years when Jesus reigns at the end of the age - or the millenium as it is commonly called.

There is much that is valid in this approach to the Bible. I only take exception to a rigid view that will not embrace some of the obvious Biblical references to the fact that God's Kingdom is a present reality.

Another problem in some believers' minds is the teaching that there is a difference between the Kingdom of God and the Kingdom of Heaven. One can settle this argument by taking a good concordance and tracing the references. The terms are interchangeable throughout the New Testament. There is no difference.

The Kingdom of God has ALWAYS been. It is the realm of God's rulership, His dominion, His power. John the Baptist cried, "Repent for the Kingdom of God is at hand (Matt. 3:2). When Jesus was here, he established the Kingdom in a new way. He said it would not be revealed through outward observation. It is in mystical form. It is here in the sense that the Holy Spirit has brought a new jurisdictional authority to the church of Jesus Christ. Now every person who lives in submission to the will of God is a part of this Kingdom.

There is little question about the future importance of God's eternal Kingdom. But if we are to displace the entrenchments of Satan in the here and now it is essential to understand Kingdom truth and authority as it relates to the present. In fact, this is what Jesus taught His disciples during his final weeks with them:

> *To whom also he showed himself alive after his passion by many infallible proofs, being seen of them forty days, and speaking of the things pertaining to the* kingdom of God. Acts 1:3

The Jewish mentality was still with the disciples. Their automatic response to the above statement of Jesus was, "Lord, will you at this time restore the kingdom to Israel?"

In a sense, Jesus glossed over their question when he answered:

> *It is not for you to know times or seasons which the Father has put in His own authority. But you shall receive power when the Holy Spirit has come upon you; and you shall be witnesses to me in Jerusalem and in Judea and Samaria, and to the end of the earth.* Acts 1:7

God's future dealings with Israel were not to be their immediate concern. His word to them was that *they* would receive authority –power –after the Holy Spirit came upon them. THEY were the ones who were going to be equipped to establish the Kingdom of God.

This was not a new idea to them. They had been introduced to the immediacy of the Kingdom of God when Jesus had taught them to pray in Matthew 6:9:

> *Our Father in heaven, hallowed be Your name. Your*
> kingdom *come. Your will be done on earth as it is*
> *in heaven. Give us this day our daily bread and forgive*
> *us our debts as we forgive our debtors. And do not lead*
> *us into temptation, but deliver us from the evil one. For*
> *yours is the* kingdom *and the power and the glory*
> *forever. Amen."*

This is a prayer of principles for day-to-day living in the Kingdom. Jesus was establishing four principles, timeless moorings upon which to anchor hope for answered prayer.

The *first principle* deals with our relationship to God –that of father-child. We are related to God through adoption.

This is explained in Romans 8:14-17:

> *" But as many as are lead by the Spirit of God, these*
> *are the sons of God. For you did not receive the spirit*
> *of bondage again to fear, but you received the Spirit of*
> *adoption by whom we cry, 'Abba, Father.' The Spirit*
> *himself bears witness with our spirit that we are*
> *children of God, and if children, then heirs - heirs of*

*God and joint heirs with Christ, if indeed we suffer with
Him, that we may also be glorified together."*

From the security of this filial position, we come boldy
before our Father with our petitions. Our confidence in prayer
is rooted in the fact of our relationship to a Father who is in
heaven.

I John 5:14 continues, "This is the confidence that we have
in him, if we ask anything according to His will, he hears us.
And if He hears us, we know that we have the petition that
we have asked of him."

Pray the promise, not the problem. God is going to give you
what you ask because He is your Father, and He loves you.
He's your Papa God.

The *second principle* in this prayer has to do with the
concept of reverential awe. God's name is to be "hallowed."
Praise and worship are involved here in revering his name.

The *third principle* has to do with authority - the authority
invested in the name of God. It is the name of Jesus that brings
God's authority down to earth.

Both the second and third principles will be discussed at
length as two of the weapons in our arsenal for warfare.

The *fourth principle* deals with rulership. "Thy Kingdom
come on earth as it is in heaven."

Many fancy twistings and turnings have been done with this
principle. Sometimes it is dismissed as a futuristic statement
but the next petitions are for the necessities of temporal
human and spiritual existence - daily bread, forgiveness of

sins, settled relationships and protection from the evil one. None of these will be required in eternal kingdom life!

The time frame of the closing words seems to make the Kingdom of God a continuum: "For thine is the kingdom and the power and the glory forever. Amen."

Now, a question may be forming in your mind. You may be thinking: "If the Kingdom of God is a present reality, and if Satan has been defeated redemptively and provisionally, then why does the Lord allow Satan the degree of latitude that he has in this church age?"

There are several reasons.

The first has to do with the attribute of God that is perfect justice. The redemptive nature of God seems to indicate that He always takes responsibility for His creation – even when it fails and falls. Although we can only speculate as to why God has permitted Satan's prolonged reign, even in dealing with this arch enemy, God will not allow the manifestation of His perfect justice to be circumvented.

Secondly, since it was man, the one God created in His own image whom Satan enticed to bring about the downfall of God's creation on earth, God is now going to use redeemed man to bring about Satan's downfall in the universe.

Again, in God's perfect if somewhat ironic sense of justice, He has chosen not to overwhelm Satan with His omnipotence. Rather, he has chosen to empower weak and foolish things of this world to overcome Satan and his kingdom (1 Corinthians 1:27).

Commissioned by the King

Third, we are being prepared to perform ministries not only in the present but in eternity. Let's look at the tri-fold ministry of the believer - that of prophet, priest and king.

(1) *Prophet*

The role of prophet is a temporary ministry for the believer (I Corinthians 13:8). For now, it serves to open the communication lines between God and man, and man and man.

The supernatural ability to speak to God through the gift of glossolalia and to transcend the barriers of human limitation by communicating to other men through the means of prophetic utterance shatters the confines of language in both the natural and spiritual realms.

Moses cried, "Oh, that all the children of the Lord would be prophets" (Numbers 11:29). Joel proclaimed that the result of the outpouring of the Spirit would be that the sons and daughters would prophecy (Joel 2:28). Paul later declared, "You all may prophecy (I Corinthians 14:31)."

(2) *Priest*

We are now, and will continue to be, worshiping priests.

> *Unto him that loved us and washed us from our sins*
> *in his own blood and hath made us* kings and priests
> *unto God and His Father, to Him be glory and domin-*
> *ion forever. Amen.*   Revelation 1:5,6

In 1 Peter 2:9,10, we are reminded that the priesthood ministry was once restricted to the covenant people of Israel. Now, however, the middle walls have been broken down and "he has made of the two a whole" (Ephesians 2:14-16).

41

Jew and Gentile have become the whole people of God, the whole Body of Christ. And with that new "wholeness" has come a new priethood and a new offering. Peter says we are now a holy nation, a royal priesthood that we should show forth the praises of God.

Our sacrifice is no longer connected with the Old Covenant, the Old Testament. All of that has been abrogated and phased out because of the work accomplished through the shedding of Jesus' blood. The alienation caused by sin has been reconciled through the redemptive work of Christ.

The sacrifice of praise and worship is what this new priesthood brings. The continuous fruit of our lips is the offering of our priesthood (Hebrews 13:15). We now come boldly before the throne of God to offer sacrifice in our priestly function.

(3) *King*

We are, and will continue to be, ruling kings, people of authority and power. The king has commissioned us to rule and reign with him.

I have already quoted Revelation 1:5,6 stating that the role of King and Priest is an appointment made by Jesus Christ Himself. The appointment to this position is a result of our adoption by God into His family and the subsequent inheritance we share as joint-heirs with Christ. (See above quotation from Romans 8.)

As one reads the fifth chapter of Romans, it becomes clear that the very purpose of Christ's death and resurrection was to deliver humanity from the slavery of sin and to make it possible for them to become ruling individuals in His Kingdom.

This idea is capsulized in the seventeenth verse: "For if by one man's offense death reigned through the one much more those who receive abundance of grace and of the gift of righteousness will reign in life through the One, Jesus Christ."

Prophet, priest, king - these functions of ministry have been committed to the Body of Christ from the time of Pentecost. If we are not prepared to perform all of them, we will be as handicapped in doing spiritual warfare as a nation would be that equipped only its land forces and ignored its air and sea units.

The King with whom we reign has not only commissioned but He has empowered and issued weaponry to His troops. We will explore the power base from which His subjects operate and we will examine individual weapons, but first, we need to be reminded of some of the decoys our enemy will use to keep us from action.

5
Diversionary Tactics

[Redeem] the time, because the days are evil.

Ephesians 5:16, KJV

Whenever Californians get sufficiently irate over the problem of smog, the powers-that-be predictably promise to do another study. The major cause has been known for years - petroleum burning motors - but in an oil producing state this presents a delicate political problem. So the studies go on!

Believers as well as many non-believers readily admit the problems of the world are caused by an evil force. As Christians we know the major cause of spiritual conflict is the one called Satan, and yet some Christians spend a lot of time doing studies on the devil. He is all out in favor of such studies! He doesn't care if we are busy formulating theorems about him. As long as such studies continue, he won't get disenfranchised.

He uses the same diversionary tactics over and over by giving them new names. At one time he convinced a segment of believers that the only way to attain a victorious spiritual life was to cloister themselves in monasteries to spend their days in contemplation. We all need to get away for periods of meditation and reflection, but when a large segment of potential Christian leaders is so isolated for a long period of time, valuable troops have been removed from the battlefield.

When faced with spiritual confrontation, Christians too often pursue a course of self-analysis rather than raising the scepter of authority against an alien foe. What is my problem, and where did it originate? What and who make me feel good about myself? What can I do about my problem - and myself? What motivates me?

"It is God's answer to the horoscope," bubbled one of our friends as she described the psychological teaching of one Christian leader. "No wonder I have been so frustrated in my Christian walk. No one ever explained to me my limitations and my strengths. It makes being a Christian so much simpler!"

No matter how sound secular psychological concepts may be they cannot replace the work of the Holy Spirit and His equipping.

At the other extreme are those who become totally absorbed in dealing with the devil through exorcism. Several Holly-

in dealing with the devil through exorcism. Several Hollywood films have popularized this approach, even to the
secular world.

There is no doubt that demons need to be cast out of some
individuals, but neither Jesus nor the disciples automatically
began to exorcise all those who came for help.

Matthew 4:24-25 records:

> *And Jesus went about all Galilee, teaching in
> their synagogues and preaching the gospel of the
> kingdom and healing all manner of disease
> among the people. And His fame went throughout
> all Syria, and they brought him all sick people
> that were taken with divers diseases and torments,
> and those that were possessed with devils, and
> those that were lunatic, and those that had palsy,
> and he healed them.*

Even in the area of healing, there was a distinction made as
to the cause of the problem. While deliverance was part of
Jesus' ministry, He did not treat every affliction as if it were
of demonic origin.

The Scriptural picture shows us that Satan and his
emissaries primarily attack the believer *externally*. By this I
mean that Satan attacks us by hurling accusations against us;
he tries to discourage, oppress, intimidate, tempt and make us
feel unworthy of our callings and stature as children of God.
But Ephesians 6:16 states that the enemy's fiery darts can be

fended off by the shield of faith. And in Revelation 12:10 we read that Satan, "the accuser of our brothers, who accused them before God day and night," will be overcome by "the blood of the Lamb and the word of their testimony."

It seems clear scripturally that the *internal* enemy of the believer is the old nature or the flesh over which victory is attained by walking in the Spirit, or putting to death these deeds of the body by the Spirit (Romans 8:13, Galatians 5). In fact, a clear listing of works of the flesh is given in Galatians 5:19-21.

Listed there are sex sins not only of practice but of desire: adultery, fornication, uncleaness (all forms of sexual perversion), lasciviousness (the partaking of anything that tends to produce lewd emotions or fosters lust and sex sins). These are all attributed to the old nature and not demon activity.

Further included in this list is witchcraft, which involves sorcery or the practice of dealing with evil spirits including the use of drugs, hallucinogens, alcohol, and potions. These all have their derivation in the fallen nature.

Some would respond by saying these sins were of the body and therefore subject to external control. They would further say that those sins that take place in the realm of the emotions or thought life are not as easily dealt with, and in fact, do need some type of exorcism.

One only needs to continue reading the Galatian list of the works of the flesh. Included are sins of the spirit such as: hatred, emulation (jealousies, uncurbed rivalry, the attempt factions, attempts to stir up trouble), strife, murders, wrath (anger, turbulent passions, indignation), revelings (partying with obscene undertones).

These internal strivings find their roots in our fallen nature which is continually at odds with the believer's new nature. The old sinful nature does not automatically dissipate when we become new creatures in Christ. Paul eloquently recorded this conflict in his experience in Romans 6 and 7. He says the things he wants to do he doesn't and vice versa. In Romans 7:24 he literally cries out, "Oh, wretched man that I am."

Every believer feels this conflict. This is the essence of the fight of faith. Paul finally came to understand that he was not a debtor to live according to the dictates of his flesh, "For," he says, "if you live according to the flesh you will die, but if by the Spirit you put to death the deeds of the body, you will live" (Romans 8:13).

This is why a confession of faith is so vital. As we quoted in Revelation 12:11, part of overcoming the works of Satan is the word of our testimony. If we do not raise that God-given shield of faith high to extinguish the enemy's fiery darts, we can be certain he will use even our own fallen natures as ammunition against us. It will always provide him something with which to accuse us!

Instead of trying to determine if the cause of a problem is their own sinful nature, some Christians believe exorcism is the only way to have Satan's influence on their lives destroyed. In their view, the sources of internal attack against stroyed. In their view, the sources of internal attack against the believer are personalized evil spirits. For example, a demon of lust, a demon of alcohol, a demon of nicotine, a spirit of fear.

I do not believe a born-again Christian can be demon-possessed. Those who believe that most or all demonic activity results in some kind of possession of the believer need to consider the following:

(1) This view nullifies the powerful, redemptive cleansing work of the blood of Christ as described in Hebrews 9:12-14:

> *Neither by the blood of goats and calves, but by his own blood, he entered once and for all into the holy place, having attained eternal redemption for us......how much more shall the blood of Christ......purge your conscience from dead works to serve the living God?*

(2) It fails to recognize the total depravity and decadence of unregenerated flesh.

> *And you hath he quickened who were dead in trespasses and sins, wherein in time past you walked according to the course of this world......fulfilling the desires of the flesh and of the mind, and were by nature the children of wrath, even as others.* Ephesians 2:1-3

(3) It ignores the rationale of the Holy Spirit who places the responsibility for "mortifying the deeds of the body" directly upon the Believer. Paul writes in Romans 8:6-8,13:

For to be carnally minded is death, but to be spiritually minded is life and peace. Because the carnal mind is enmity against God, for it is not subject to the law of God, nor indeed can be. So then those who are in the flesh cannot please God. For if you live according to the flesh you will die, but if by the Spirit you put to death the deeds of the body, you will live. For as many as are led by the Spirit of God, these are the sons of God.

(4) Personalizing evil spirits has been given impetus by using examples such as "the spirit of fear" mentioned in 2 Timothy 1:7 and "a spirit of infirmity" in Luke 13:11.

If one were to personalize a spirit of fear, then to accurately interpret grammatically, one would also have to have a personal spirit of power, a personal spirit of love and a personal spirit of soundness of mind. Logically, then if one could exorcise the spirit of fear, one could also call upon good personal spirits to inhabit where one had been demonized.

The most casual Bible student would have difficulty with this explanation. Good scholarship has always interpreted these to be attitudes, and there are hundreds of scriptures which would substantiate this view.

The Weapons of our Warfare

There is no doubt that sickness and disease are the works of the enemy. It is one of his favorite weapons to use in attack against the temple of the Holy Spirit which is our physical body (1 Corinthians 6:19). But to say that the spirit of infirmity that Jesus loosed the woman from in Luke 13:10-16 was some kind of internalized demonic presence does not hold up in the light of what he did. Jesus laid his hands on the woman, loosed her from her infirmity and "immediately she was made straight and glorified God." He did not cast out the devil nor speak to demons as he often did when exorcizing them.

Paul first preached the gospel to the Galatians through infirmity of the flesh (Galatians 4:13). To the Corinthians he wrote, "If I must needs glory, I will glory of the things that concern my infirmities" (2 Corinthians 11:30).

There are those who say Paul would not have been troubled with infirmities if he had properly understood faith. Such a statement seems arrogant when one considers Paul received the highest revelation of God ever given to a man (2 Corinthians 12:2-4).

Even if there were a grain of truth in such a ridiculous charge, one certainly cannot imagine the Apostle Paul being so lacking in faith that he "gloried" in being "demonized" by a spirit of infirmity.

For the believer, the very sober question must be answered. If one were to die with an unexorcized demon dwelling in the soul, where would one go? Certainly, the demon could not enter heaven, and if the soul could not enter heaven, it would mean that the blood of Christ and the continual cleansing of the believer as described in I John 1:9, "If we confess our sin he is faithful and just to forgive us our sin and to cleanse us from all unrighteousness," was not enough to deliver one from the bondage of Satan.

The notion that a demonic presence could inhabit the soul but not the spirit of an individual is an ancient idea. The ecclesiastical name for it is Fragmentation and it defines the severe partitioning of body, soul and spirit into separate entities. It is a pagan concept which has always been rejected as heresy by orthodox scholarship. It is the basis of such cultic practices as levitation, spirit migration, walking on coals of fire, laying on spiked beds, etc.

Satan is delighted with all the attention he gets! If he can get a believer expending his spiritual energies fighting him on ground Christ has already conquered, he not only is able to discredit the redemptive work of Christ, but he keeps one's focus off the real battle that needs to be fought.

6
Gearing Up!

Finally, my brethren, be strong in the Lord and in the power of His might.
Ephesians 6:10, NKJ

"**F**inally" - it's a word of summation, a signal that one is reaching a culmination point. What is Paul referring to as he moves into this classic instruction on warfare. What precedes "finally?"

Ephesians has commonly been called the Alps of the New Testament because of the high doctrinal content contained in the first four chapters. Almost as a nonsequitor sandwiched between the lofty teaching on the church and the ending call to warfare are the most basic instructions for interpersonal relationships. Paul reasons that if your doctrine is sound your

55

relationships must also be sound. The evidence that one is in right relationship to heavenly authority is the fact that he is in right relationship with others. When both are right, then you are ready to arm for warfare.

The instructions on relationships center around a word that is almost foreign to macho Western thought - SUBMIT!

"But, Paul," one may reasonably ask, "Submission means giving in. Is that any way to prepare for war?"

The answer is yes. Jesus explained this apparent paradox in his discussion with the Centurion who was seeking healing for his servant (Matthew 8). When Jesus volunteered to "come and heal him", the Centurion demurred explaining, "Lord, I am not worthy that you should come under my roof. But only speak a word, and my servant shall be healed. For I also am a man under authority, having soldiers under me. And I say to this one, 'Go' and he goes; and to another, 'Come', and he comes. And to my servant, 'Do this,' and he does it."

"When Jesus heard it, He marveled and said to those who followed, "Assuredly, I say to you, I have not found such great faith, not even in Israel!"

The principle spelled out here is that in order to be in authority, one must first have learned to come under authority. The Centurion knew that whatever command he himself gave to his subordinates would be carried out exactly as he wished. To have such power, however, he had first submitted himself to the authority of the Roman Empire. In turn it had rewarded him by placing him in control of his troops. The Centurion assumed that God had likewise given Jesus the same power.

His comprehension of the authority structure of the Kingdom of God so pleased Jesus that he commended the Roman officer's faith above any that he had found in Israel - the depository of God's dealing for generations!

Paul teaches that we need to have a submissive spirit in five areas of relationship:

(1) Submission **to** the Holy Spirit.

> *And do not be drunk with wine in which is dissipation, but be filled with the Spirit.*
>
> Ephesians 5:17

Submission to the Holy Spirit is critical if you are to fight spiritual warfare. He brings to us the inner witness as to how we should participate in holy living. He guides us as we establish right priorities. Successful warfare cannot be waged if you are grieving the Holy Spirit.

There is an interesting comparison here between wine and being filled with the Spirit. Drunkenness brought on by drinking wine is a means of escape. It produces temporary relaxation and hilarity.

Warfare is a dreary pursuit. In order to keep the morale high among fighting men and take the drudgery out of training, all sorts of diversions are used - marching bands, service songs, competitions.

Our Heavenly Commander has not overlooked the need for spiritual warriors to maintain a strong sense of camaraderie. Rather than the escape of drunkenness, it is the Holy Spirit with His bundle of gifts that elevates the spirit of those engaged in battle.

As we submit to the Holy Spirit, we submit also to the Comforter, the Helper, the Healer, the Divine Morale Builder. He is the one who walks beside, who leads, who guides, who directs, who prepares a table before us even in the presence of our enemies.

(2) Submission to one another

> *Speaking to one another in psalms and hymns and spiritual songs, ... submitting to one another in the fear of God.* Ephesians 5:19-21

There is nothing quite like spiritual fellowship. This admonition not only sounds spiritual, but sounds like a lot of fun!

If we fail to understand the absolute necessity of properly relating to other Christians, we will never be able to function as warriors. The "Lone Ranger" spirit in a Christian indicates an ignorance of the infrastructure of believers in the Kingdom of God. God requires that none of us thinks too highly of ourselves. In fact, Jesus told us in His kingdom, "The first will be last and the last will be first."

Imagine how gruesome it would be to walk outside and find a severed hand lying on the lawn. That hand, a vital element when connected to its owner's body would be useless there on the lawn. Similarly, although Christians are individual members of the Body of Christ, we must be connected to the rest of the Body to function effectively as Christians.

58

Gearing Up!

As we move to the end of this age, the spirit of the world will be characterized by lawlessness and anarchy. Professing Christians who are in rebellion to leaders and who will not submit to one another will be the ones who are destroyed by deception or, at the least, rendered totally ineffectual.

(3) Submission of wives to husbands, and husbands responsibilities to wives.

> *Wives submit to your own husbands as to the Lord. For the husband is head of the wife, as also Christ is head of the church and He is the Savior of the body. Therefore, just as the church is subject to Christ, so let the wives be to their own husbands in everything. Husbands, love your wives, just as Christ also loved the church and gave Himself for it ......So husbands ought to love their own wives as their own bodies, he who loves his wife loves himself. For no one ever hated his own flesh, but nourishes and cherishes it, just as the Lord does the church.*
>
> Ephesians 5:22-29

A married couple will never become effective in spiritual warfare if there is an imbalance in their marriage. And there will be an imbalance if the Biblical concept of submission is not an integral part of the marriage. Too often strong responsibility has fallen upon the wife to make the relationship work - by *her* act of submission.

While one partner cannot be responsible for the success of the marriage relationship, Paul teaches that the primary burden rests with the husband to love his wife as Christ loved the Church. He is to be her covering. He is to give himself sacrifically for her. He is to sanctify (set apart) and cleanse her in a healing sense. Most wives would agree that submission to that kind of husband would come easily!

First Peter 3:7 elaborates on the husband's role:

Likewise you husbands, dwell with them in under-standing, giving honor to the wife, as to the grace of life, that your prayers may not be hindered.

If a couple's spiritual life is to have impact and their prayers are to be effective, the husband must treat his wife as a "co-heir." There are no second-class citizens in the Kingdom of God. The most beautiful example of the arrangement of submission is to be found in the Godhead itself: Father, Son and Holy Spirit—a horizontal, integrated union.

As a pastor I cannot disconnect my marriage relationship from my ministry. It can't be done! Sooner or later failure in marriage would defeat me and my ministry. If my prayer life were cut off and God were not answering my prayers because of neglect in my marriage, how in the world would I have power to wage spiritual warfare?

(4) Submission of children to parents.

Children obey your parents in the Lord, for this is right. "Honor your father and mother," which is

Gearing Up!

the first commandment with promise, "that it may
be well with you and you may live long on the
earth. And you fathers, do not provoke your
children to wrath but bring them up in the training
and admonition of the Lord.

Ephesians 6:1-4 NKJ

A right relationship between children and parents is required if the family is to wage effective warfare against Satan. Without it the family becomes a prime target for the enemy.

Prior to praying for persons to be healed, quite often I ask them if they have honored their parents. I especially pursue this if it seems like a tough case where we are getting no answers. When I first began doing this, it came as a surprise how many of them would acknowledge that there was bitterness and sometimes hatred in their hearts toward their parents.

In this day of divorce, abandonment and assorted abuses, this should not have come as a surprise. There are deep wounds that fester even in the hearts of mature believers. Before the throne of God, these relationships can be made right - even if the parent is dead. When animosity is released in forgiveness, God heals the broken hearts and makes the lives go well.

As parents we must walk the path between the extremes of of being too autocratic or being too permissive. I cannot come down on my children so harshly that they do not receive an understanding of grace. By provoking them to wrath, they will reject both me and my God. However, if I do not take the time to train and admonish them in the way they should go, their undisciplined behavior will disqualify or seriously dissipate the effectiveness of our family as a spiritual force.

(5) Submission of servants to masters.

> *Servants, be obedient to those who are your masters according to the flesh, with fear and trembling, in sincerity of heart, as to Christ. Not with eyeservice, as men-pleasers, but as servants of Christ......And you, masters, do the same things to them, giving up threatening, knowing that your own Master also is in heaven and there is no partiality with Him.*
>
> *Eph. 6:4-9*

While in our present culture, this admonition would be more appropriate for employee-employer or labor relationships, the teaching is very practical. If you are working for someone and take advantage of your boss, if you are rebellious and a troublemaker on the job, you will not be an effective spiritual soldier.

When I was teaching at LIFE Bible College in Southern California, some students could not resist the urge to take time off from their outside jobs and spend the day at the beach. On more than one occasion, a student would get a deep sunburn, but still report back to his employer the next day with the excuse they had been sick.

Often the employers who had been gracious in working with the student placement service, would complain that they did not think our student was acting as one should who was preparing for ministry. And they were right! Students who practiced that kind of deception and lack of integrity and carried it into their ministries were going to find themselves impaired spiritually.

Paul challenges employers as well. If you are an employer you are to remember that you are under a heavenly Master. Even though you are in a position of authority, you cannot be heavy-handed in your administration. If your employee is a Christian, you must understand that he or she is also a brother or sister. An unbelieving employee is to be shown the love of Christ. Christian employers are never to take advantage of those who work for them. They must provide just wages and working conditions. Favoritism of any kind is forbidden and fairness is required.

Why does the Holy Spirit place such strong emphasis on relationships before telling us how to put the hosts of hell to flight? There are two reasons:

First, it makes sense that relationships should be strengthened before one goes into combat. It frees the soldier from disconcerting anxieties about the home front. If all relationships have been secured there, the warrior can approach the battle without diversion.

Secondly, Paul says in Ephesians 6:15, that our feet are to

be shod with the gospel of peace. Everywhere we go, we are to minister the peace of Jesus to people. We are to calm troubled hearts and proclaim the good news of God's love. We are to be ministers of reconciliation.

We cannot be this if we do not examine our feelings and motives regarding people. We have to make certain of what spirit we are. Are we going to bless people or are we going to curse them?

When Jesus picked up the scroll of Isaiah and began to read, He stopped in the middle of a sentence. He omitted the last phrase written by Isaiah that the Messiah would proclaim the "day of his wrath and judgment." A number of scholars believe that this was not an oversight on the part of Jesus (after all, He was the Living Word), but that since his advent we are not living in a time of proclaiming wrath and judgment. In this "day of grace" as it has come to be called, we are to proclaim the acceptable year of the Lord when all debts are cancelled, the prison houses are opened, and the prisoners are set free. Certainly, this kind of grace characterized both the ministry of Jesus and the writings of the Apostle Paul. The Gospel call is, "Be reconciled to God, for God is reconciled to you."

In 1984 there was widespread interest among the Christian community of Southern California in a prophecy that had been given by a couple who had a long history of credible ministry. The prophecy said there would be a devastating earthquake during the Olympic games. Detailed instructions of how to prepare and survive it were printed and widely distributed.

Gearing Up!

When a copy reached me, I could not believe it, not so much because I thought the prophets were false, but because it did not fit in with what God has called us to be at this time - ministers of reconciliation. To make Southern California the object of His wrath toward our sinfulness would mean that not only this geographical area, but the world, had crossed the line from acceptable year of the Lord to the day of His wrath.

Certainly the day of His wrath will come. God will allow, and even be the efficient cause of this pouring out of judgment, but wicked as it may be, Southern California will not be the only area to experience it. The book of Revelation describes that time as a period when sin will manifest itself completely as the rebellion led by the anti-Christ is unleashed in all the earth.

Until that time, God has committed to us a gospel of peace and reconciliation. This is why it is all important that our relationships with other Christians, members of our family and members of the community-at-large be kept in scriptural perspective.

Now, we have come full circle, back to the word with which we began - *finally*. *Finally*, we are ready for warfare. *Finally*, we will see God's power released, and the enemy defeated *–Finally!*

7

The Spirit
of the Warrior

*Do you not know that those who run in a
race all run, but one receives the prize?
Run in such a way that you may obtain it.*

1 Corinthians 9:24, NKJ

Space is the new frontier of discovery for mankind. It has
the challenge of being the last unknown for man to explore.

Thousands of persons have the curiosity, the educational
background, the physical ability, and the technical knowledge
to venture into space, but from those thousands, only a few
score of men and women are called to make the assault. It
takes more than skill and abilities to become one of the select
group who qualify.

The Weapons of our Warfare

In his book and the subsequent movie Tom Wolfe described what is considered to be THE RIGHT STUFF for astronauts. Beyond learned abilities and physical prowess, the people who have "the right stuff" must also have the right spirit. Wolfe writes about the exceptional qualities that motivated the extraordinary men who first broke through the earth's atmosphere.

The first obvious characteristic was their insatiable desire for pioneering. They were not interested in pursuing what someone else had already accomplished. They wanted to do what no one else had done before. It was almost an obsession with them - to be the fastest men in the world, to cross another unconquered barrier. They wanted to break through thresholds of discovery. They were never satisfied with status quo. Their motivation was to be on the cutting edge of the new wave of adventure - regardless of danger.

Another quality that typified these people, was their positive attitude toward the space project. They never gave into the possibility of failure in their thinking. They were always of the opinion that they were going to make it - they were going to do it. There WERE failures but their attitudes never changed. They wanted new records to break, and they were not afraid to risk reaching out to break them.

Right-stuff people never seemed to be discouraged by the immediate circumstances. They went through physical and mental preparation that seemed intolerable then, and ridiculous now. With the choosing of each new team, there was potential for jealousy and frustration among the ones not selected. Whatever their personal discomfort, or discontent, they did not waver in their commitment to be prepared for the final goal - going into space.

Right-stuff people do not panic under pressure! All of the astronauts were subjected to G-forces that distorted their bodies with agonizing pain. They had to be able to ignore the pain and concentrate on the job at hand - flying their craft. So cool were these men under pressure, that the famed test pilot, Chuck Yeager, was once monitored as having all his vital signs functioning normally even as the experimental plane he was flying disintegrated around him!

This right- stuff spirit is not confined to space pioneers. In sports, numbers of persons have overcome handicaps that all the experts said were unconquerable.

Wilma Rudolph, born with club feet, became one of the top gold medal winners in Olympic history for women's track events. Mark Spitz, devastated by rheumatic fever in childhood, fought back to win seven gold medals in swimming. O. J. Simpson overcame severe bowing in his legs by rickets to become one of the top running backs in professional football. Likewise, Rocky Blier, with half of his foot shot off in the Viet Nam war became a record-setting running back for the Pittsburgh Steelers.

Millions of viewers lost their hearts to a star of the 1984

Olympics. Randy Lewis cut down in the peak of his ability by leukemia came back to win a gold medal for wrestling.

Possessing the right stuff, need not be the shining quality of astronauts and athletes alone. If women and men in their natural, human spirit can rise to conquer such challenges, we who are reinforced by the Holy Spirit should accept no limitations to the potential for great conquest that God has projected for each of us.

Many pastors have never known the thrill of victory because they have been content to settle for an "also ran" position. If things don't work out in one place, they shuffle off to another assignment to see if the track is faster over there. They seem oblivious to the fact that there is a vast frontier that needs to be assaulted and subdued for the Kingdom of God outside the front door of *any* church.

Sometimes we go through things we do not understand as God prepares us to enter new frontiers. We may undergo rigorous training in some forsaken place on the back side of the desert. We believe God led us there, but we don't see any purpose in it. It may be rough, and all hell seems to be breaking loose. Maybe the preparation seems intolerable, or even ridiculous, and everyone - including God - is passing over you.

There was a time when I was in a constant pity party. Whatever I talked about with regard to ministry was a confession of defeat. Of course, it was always someone else's fault

- my supervisor, my denomination, my congregation, my finances. Even when there were victories, I did not appreciate their sweetness because there was always someone or something which did not live up to my expectations.

The Bible teaches over and over that our mouths, which convey our attitudes, can completely frustrate and negate the victory in which God wants us to live. Proverbs 18:21 says that the power of life and death is in the tongue. If one gives into verbal negativity, saying things that do not give credit to the potential of your life in Christ – it will nullify even the good and victorious things that God does.

There has to be a mentality of commitment in the spiritual warrior. He has to learn to stick it out, to hang in there, and keep the ultimate goal of invading and defeating the enemy foremost in his mind. The Lord hasn't passed one over permanently. He allows these specific experiences to bring us to a place where we know what it means to have the right stuff in His Kingdom.

There are many famous examples of intrepid spiritual warriors, but the ones which inspire me the most come from the rank and file believers whom I have been privileged to know over the years.

A woman, whom I shall rename Alice for purposes of this story, came to know Jesus as her Savior in her mid-thirties. Her life had revolved around her family and home. Love for her Savior brought new focus to her life, and soon she found herself torn between her husband's wishes and her desire to be a Godly person. To describe him as a swinger was an understatement, and her life became almost unbearable as she tried to maintain her balance as a good wife and a good Christian.

She spent many hours weeping before the Lord, not because she felt sorry for herself but because she was tenaciously interceeding before Him for the salvation of her husband. One day she came to my office from the prayer room. "I can't take it any more," she cried, "The more I pray, the more abusive he gets."

More to comfort her than to ask help for her husband I suggested we pray one more time. As we were praying, she saw in a vision a ten foot wide brick wall. It was so high she could not see over it. As she stood before it, she saw piles of bricks from the layers she had broken through, but to her dismay there was always another layer to be torn down.

"How wide is this wall?" she asked the Lord. "I will never have the strength to keep tearing it down. I'll just have to give up!" She said she was suddenly elevated to the top of the wall and there she saw that one solitary layer of bricks stood between her and a beautiful wooded meadow.

"I'm going to make it," she smiled. Several months later as she prepared to leave with her children for Sunday School her husband appeared in the doorway dressed in his best suit. When asked where he was going he casually replied, "To church with you and the kids!" He came, he gave his life to

The Spirit of the Warrior

Jesus, and they've been serving Him together ever since.

She later told the story, "That last layer fell down without a sound. I didn't know it had crumbled. How glad I am I didn't give up on that brick wall!"

The spiritual warrior at times undergoes G-pressures that seem as if they will blow him apart. His life may become totally distorted from all meaningful perspective.

The right stuff does not panic under Satan's G-forces. This is the time to ignore the pain and soar on wings of the Spirit so that control will come back to our craft of faith. His Word says it will happen - the authority of hell will not, cannot, prevail against the authority of the Kingdom of God. God has given us mighty weapons to tear down the strongholds of Satan. We are not controlled by Satan. HIS activity is controlled by us!

The terrible possibility remains, however, that one can escape the pain of such pressure by jumping from one testing ground to another. If we do, we will never be prepared to pass the final test that qualifies us for flight into the heavenly realms of conquest.

The right stuff sits tight or in Biblical terms, stands still and sees the salvation of the Lord. If we really are authority people, if we are in places where God has put us, we must accept one of these options: Either (1) God is helpless or has put Himself in such a limited position that there is no way He can help me overcome the hindering forces in my life. Or (2)

God is what He says He is, and will do what He says He will do.

Why in the world would God send us to fight foes who could not be defeated. It would make no sense for us to be defeated by them and become subject to their pressures.

On the contrary, in the Kingdom of God it is a disgrace and source of deep sorrow when a child of God fails. It is a disservice to the grace of God. It is an affront to the power of the Holy Spirit. IT IS UNACCEPTABLE.

No Christian should ever be satisfied with status quo conditions. There is always ground to be taken, battles to be won, victories to be relished. The spirit of the Christian warrior is continually experiencing the risk of reaching into new territory.

In the San Diego area where I now minister, there has never been a major revival. The last major move of God was in 1925 when Aimee Semple McPherson held a crusade. One of her plans to draw a crowd was to preach from a prize ring erected on the stage. Her opponent was - the devil! Thousands of people came to see this great evangelist and thousands of people made decisions for Christ.

The arena has broadened, but the opponent remains the same. God has put a rod up my back. I want the authority of the Kingdom of God to prevail in this area. I want the rulers of wickedness in this area defeated. I want to run to win - to receive the prize of a tremendous spiritual breakthrough   that will once again liberate thousands into the Kingdom of God.   The Holy Spirit is saying -

Don't panic!

Don't retreat!

And having done all, stand (Eph. 6:13)

8
Battle Strategy

For we do not wrestle against flesh and blood, but against principalities, against powers, against the rulers of the darkness of this age, against spiritual hosts of wickedness in heavenly places.

Ephesians 6:12, NKJ

In describing the kind of warfare that we engage in, Paul uses an interesting word –*wrestle*. Wrestling is not a team endeavor - not the work of a platoon or company, but an individual effort. This doesn't mean that one's walk of faith is a solo endeavor. Paul states previously in Galatians 6 that we are to bear one another's burdens. One brother described it well when he said, "When you're close enough to the Body

77

of Christ, it's difficult to fall because the other members are so tightly knit they hold one another up."

Yet the progress of spiritual growth is each individual's responsibility. For the long haul, I can't carry your pack, and you can't carry mine.

One of the great frailties of the church has been that so many of the laity believe that all ministry should be centered in the clergy. On the national as well as local levels the church has developed star systems. For example, there are members of congregations who will not be satisfied with ministry from any one but the Senior Pastor or someone they regard as having the most prestige.

We are hearing and seeing more and more that the Lord is pulling this kind of security blanket away from His people and saying, "Each of you needs to come into ministry. Each of you needs to share in the triumphant life of Jesus. *Every* soldier must learn to fight effectual warfare."

When our sons were growing up, one of their favorite topics of discussion was what they were going to buy when they were old enough to be on their own. Occasionally we would say, "Well, be sure to save enough to pay for groceries, utilities, rent, taxes, gasoline, insurance...."

One day Joel looked at us seriously and said, "I think I'll just stay a kid!"

The hard thing about coming into maturity is that it brings responsibility. Like Joel, some Christians look at the responsibility entailed with warfare - and decide to remain a spiritual kid. But back to wrestling those formidable spiritual opponents!

Our boys loved to watch wrestling on television. In my view, it is a silly form of entertainment. Each wrestler creates a more flamboyant outfit and personality than the next. His popularity depends on how well he captures the audience's fancy. The matches are scripted and staged to get the maximum audience.

Orthodox wrestling on the other hand is so slow and laborious only the most dedicated fans would watch it. One hold can last ten minutes. In order to make wrestling appealing to a general audience, it has to revolve around theatrics.

There is a lesson here! Our warfare is not always a dramatic flip and pin. Sometimes the devil gets us in a hold that seems to last and last. We become weary and want to concede the point.

This is the time for perseverance of faith that will not let go. Jacob learned this lesson. His enemy was closing in on him. The New King James version picks up the story: "Then Jacob was left alone; and a Man wrestled with him until breaking of day. Now when He saw that He did not prevail against him, He touched the socket of his hip; and the socket of Jacob's hip was out of joint as He wrestled with him. And He said, "I will not let You go unless You bless me!" (Genesis 32:24-26).

Can you imagine the anguish of that hold, the pain of the

dislocated hip? But Jacob hung on - and was blessed.

Jesus Himself applauded tenancity of spirit in the story he told about the friend coming at midnight to borrow bread (Luke 11:5-8).

The householder was settled in for a nice comfortable night with his family. He and his family were all snuggled down in cozy, warm beds - and here comes the knock.

"Wake up in there, neighbor. I've got some people who are visiting me. I need bread." Knock, Knock, *bang*. "Please get up. I've got to borrow some bread!"

Jesus explains the point of the story. The householder is not going to get up for friendship sake. By this time, the friendship was definitely strained. But, in order to get rid of him so his family can go back to sleep, he finally gets up and gives him the bread.

Jesus goes on to say, "And I say to you, ask, and it will be given to you. Seek and you will find. Knock and it will be opened unto you."

He continues by saying that if our earthly fathers, being evil, know how to give good gifts, shall not our heavenly Father much more give us what we ask.

There is a fine line that is drawn here in our wrestling match with Satan. Our persistence in the struggle is not based upon our own strength or ability to break the enemy's hold. Our persistence is based upon our absolute confidence that the enemy's strength has already been dissipated and that we have been declared the winners.

Battle Strategy

And you, being dead in your trespasses and the uncircumcision of your flesh, He has made alive together with Him, having forgiven you all trespasses, having wiped out the handwriting of requirements that was against us, which was contrary to us. And He has taken it out of the way, having nailed it to the cross. Having disarmed principalities and powers, he made a public spectacle of them, triumphing over them in it.

Colossians 2:12-15

What does that mean? The same thing it meant to Israel when they entered the promised land. The land had been given to them by covenant agreement with God. But it didn't become their actual possession until they stepped forward to claim it.

Our covenant for possession has been ratified by the blood of Jesus. Spiritual victory can be established, however, only as we move in and appropriate the provisions of the new covenant. If we don't fight for it, we won't displace the enemy. He will not move from his squatter's quarters until we command him to go.

How do we get the spiritual gumption, nerve, fortitude, strength - call it what you will - to go in and rout the enemy? The secret is in the commissioning verse of Ephesians 6:

"Finally, my brethren, be strong in the Lord, and in the *powr of His might*" (v. 10).

The Weapons of Our Warfare

In addition to the confidence that comes with the legal provisions of the new covenant, the great qualifier for spiritual warfare is the Holy Spirit - the power of His might.

Jesus told the disciples they were not to move one foot out of Jerusalem until they had received the power of the Holy Spirit. So convinced were the members of the early Church that the empowering of the Holy Spirit was needed, they sought out even for menial jobs in serving food and for minor administrative work men who were "full of wisdom and full of the Holy Spirit" (Acts 6:3).

Stephen, one of the chosen servants, was a young Hellenist who had been a participant in the outpouring of the Holy Spirit. He had no calling to specific ministry it would seem, but was recognized by the brethren as one on whom they could place responsibility.

Little did he know that his equipping for service would enable him to become the strong witness who would open the eyes of Saul who would become Apostle Paul. And it was Stephen, full of wisdom and the Holy Spirit, who became the first battle casualty of the early church.

Heroes of the faith, Biblical or otherwise, are not individuals who have seen themselves as persons destined for heroism. They are people marked by obedience to God, commitment to the task He has assigned them, and quite often, they have been the only ones to "fill the gap." Diligence to small responsibilities is the growing ground for great faith, and consequently great victories. Our spiritual muscles may become sore as we begin to work out in preparation for the tasks the Lord has called us to, but the strength will come for us to become wrestlers who always win the matches of life.

9
Choose
Your Weapons

Put on the whole armor of God, that you may be able to stand against the wiles of the devil.

Ephesians 6:11, NKJ

Nothing could be more logical - could it? If we are being commanded in God's Word to fight, then we will be issued protective armor and weaponry. The word "wiles" has primarily to do with strategies. In the military sense, it means a fighting unit has a deliberately planned strategy.

The way we are going to outmaneuver our enemy, Paul advises, will be by putting on the whole armor of God. As Christians, we are issued equipment that will devastate the wiles of the devil —no matter how calculated or well–planned his strategies are.

I have known people who are certain that the devil is out to steal, destroy and kill, but they are not so certain that they can do anything about it. As I have previously said, they take a fatalistic que sera sera, whatever-will-be-will-be attitude, and they never bother to pick up a weapon with which to counter attack. Like Stuart Barnes, they don't want to upset the enemy, hoping he won't bother them.

If believers were not to engage in warfare, why are we being told to be strong in the Lord and in the power of His might? Why are we issued armor? Why are we equipped for battle?

The weaponry that we want to check out is the "basic issue" described in the sixth chapter of Ephesians: girding or belt, breastplate, shoes, shield, helmet and sword. First we want to look at the badge or insignia worn on our spiritual uniform.

When I was in college, I worked for a bank located on the corner of Fourth and Main in downtown Los Angeles. At that time Chief Parker was the head of the Los Angeles Police Department. A former two-star general in the Marine Corps, he had carried the spit-and-polish discipline from the Corps into the police force. Everything that was supposed to to shine, shone. Every crease was pressed to perfection. The white hats and gloves were spotless.

They were a self-confident crew as they stood in the inter-sections of downtown Los Angeles. Without looking around, they would blow their whistles, hold up a gloved hand, and every vehicle or pedestrian did exactly what was required. They were fearless as they stood without protection in the middle of dense traffic.

Physically, they were no more invincible than other pedestrians. The source of their confidence had to do with the badge they proudly displayed on their hats and shirts. It indicated they were officers of the law commissioned by the City of Los Angeles. When they put up their hands, the entire city - the citizens, the government officials, the legal system - stood behind them with all their collective authority.

Although the badge of authority may seem to be a passive piece of equipment, without it the police officers were merely men in blue uniforms. The badge indicated that they were invested with every power necessary to perform their duties. Likewise, without the badge of spiritual authority we will be unable to control the enemy's activities, let alone destroy him.

There are two words that describe the kind of authority that has been given to the believer.

The Greek word dunamis has to do with intrinsic power. Our word dynamite is derived from this word. We might say it is explosive power. It also has to do with virtue and ability. This is is the power Jesus told His disciples to wait for in Jerusalem. The Lord was saying that when He poured out His spirit on His followers, He was going to give them access to His virtue along with the intrinsic strength of

His power.

The other Greek word that is used in connection with authority is exousia. This refers to a delegated authority such as comes with the power of attorney and it works like this: My mother has been an invalid for years, and for years, I have carried her power of attorney. It means she has delegated her authority to manage her finances to me. When I show that document, my requests on her behalf are automatically honored.

As Christians we have been given delegated authority to set the boundaries on Satan's activities. When we hold up our badge, our document of authority which is the Word of God, he must comply.

We do not have to be intimidated by Satan. We have been delegated authority by the Ruler of the Universe. When we hold up our hand, when Satan sees our badge, when we resist him, he has to accept our authority - and be gone.

This is not presumptious faith. It is not being afraid to wear the badge of God's authority. Like the self-confident police officer, it is having the confidence that God Himself has commissioned you to raise His insignia in the intersections of life.

And the enemy can quickly identify the genuine badge of authority. Trying to duplicate Paul's ministry by their own efforts, the sons of Sceva were overpowered and wounded by an evil spirit. "Jesus I know, and Paul I know, but who are you?" the evil spirit taunted them (Acts 19:14).

The Christian who understands that all victory over the enemy has been won by the Lord Jesus will never be defeated. Jesus will give us the authority to proclaim and stand in the confidence of that completed work. It is when we begin to look at our own weaknesses, our own failures, our own sins, that we lose courage. We begin to feel we are not worthy to wear the badge, to put on the armor, to engage the weapons.

Satan will continually try to discourage us and undermine our confidence in the redemptive work of Jesus by tempting us to place our confidence in ourselves rather than Him.

Somebody said, "You do not have to attribute Jesus' great wisdom to some kind of anointing that came upon him when he was just a kid of twelve and was confounding professors in the synagogue. Just imagine what he had going for him –He was sinless!"

Occasionally, we get a small glimpse of what the original creation must have been before sin marred mankind. We see it in the genius of an Einstein or a Whiz Kid like Joel Kupperman who could compute college calculus when he was six years old.

Paderewski was giving concerts and had composed sixteen pieces by the time he was eight years old. It is said of him that he didn't want to play or do anything that would take him away from the keyboard and that his mother had to force him to go out to play with other children. There was a spirit of genius about him that separated him from others.

We pondered this gift of musical genius when we were forcing our own children to practice their piano lessons! "How much easier it would be for them - and us - if they could be imbued with a bit of Paderewski's spirit," we would lament.

In the realm of Christian experience, this is a striking comparison. We have been imbued with God's spirit yet so often we shrink in fear, or wallow in feelings of unworthiness, when we contemplate aggressive spiritual life. When told we should confront the enemy and drive him from the land, it seems such a dreary, impossible task. It is so much easier to sit in the safe enclaves of our traditional religious practices.

If fear or defeatism or lethargy paralyzes you in this manner pray for the Spirit of the Lord to come upon YOU. Pray for courage and boldness to confront the enemy. Pray for a renewing of your mind to anticipate the battle simply because we know we can anticipate the triumphant outcome!

The weapons? They are all at our disposal, proven and tested by the Quartermaster of Heaven. He has never lost a battle and he knows exactly what is needed to put the enemy to flight in every circumstance.

The Word of God, The Name of Jesus, The Blood of Jesus, Prayer and Fasting, Gifts of the Spirit, Praise and Worship, Binding and Loosing. What an armory - everything we need to drive the enemy from the land.

Choose Your Weapons

We have scouted the enemy's camp. We have secured the home front by putting our relationships in order. We have tested our own will to do battle. We have been commissioned and given the badge of authority by our Commander. He in turn has given us His spirit and ability. Now it's time to learn to use the weapons.

10
The Blood
of Jesus

"Knowing that you were not redeemed with corruptible things, like silver or gold, from your aimless conduct received by tradition from your fathers, but with the precious blood of Christ, as of a lamb without blemish and without spot."

I Peter 1:18-19

Before we consider the blood of Jesus as a weapon in spiritual warfare, let's look at it from a universal perspective. First, think of the magnitude of our universe.

Since I live near the Mt. Palomar observatory, I recently saw a picture taken with its 200-inch telescope that shows the black holes located in space. Astronomers do not really understand these holes except that they seem to have an infinite depth of blackness and seem infinite in their dimensions. The immensity of all that is out there is incomprehensible even to scientists with sophisticated equipment.

The Scriptures speak of "outer darkness" (Matthew 8:12). They also talk about three heavens - the atmospheric heaven of our earth, the galactic heaven and the third heaven. Right now the third heaven is the abode of Jesus in His glorified body.

Some people worry about being bored in heaven. They have conjured up a picture of angel-like persons floating around on clouds strumming harps. That doesn't sound very exciting! What seems nearer the truth is that we will be set free in unlimited creativity. Eternally, God will open vistas of understanding into the universe as we now know it - and even into what lies beyond.

Now with all the expanse and mysteries of the universe to be contemplated, what do we consider the most valuable, the most precious commodity in the vastness of the universe?

I once asked this question of a Bible Study group. They named a variety of things, but finally agreed that "life" would be their answer. And I agree, what good is anything without life? It has the ability to be conscious and self-conscious. It has the ability to feel internal things and recognize external things. It can discern things and make distinctions. This ability to understand and analyze gives human life its supremacy.

Then what is the one thing that makes life possible? Leviticus 17:11 tells us that the life of the flesh is in the blood.

If we understand that the most important thing in the

universe is life - and that life is in the blood - then we begin to understand Peter's statement at the beginning of this chapter about the preciousness of the blood of Jesus.

The blood of Jesus was GOD'S life! No wonder it became the redemptive price for our sins. Is there anything more valuable in this entire, immense universe?

The late Dr. H. R. De Haan in his book, *The Chemistry of the Blood*, contended that the blood of Jesus was chemically the same as other human blood, but it was totally different in that there was no corruptive element in it.

I believe that Jesus had to submit to crucifixion on the cross because otherwise he would have lived forever. There was no sin in Him so there was no death in Him. He said, "No man taketh my life from me. I give it" (John 10:17-18).

In comparison to the blood of Christ, all other substances are corrupt. We have been redeemed with the only incorruptible substance in the universe - the life of God which was flowing in the veins of the sinless Messiah.

Some theologians will say the virgin birth is an optional tenet of faith. But the virgin birth is absolutely crucial to understanding the efficacy of Jesus' sacrificial offering.

Not conceived by a human father, but interjected by the Holy Spirit was the divine spermatos that produced the fetus of the Christ child. Prepared in the womb of that Jewish teenager was a completely different breed of human life. It was to be the prototype of a whole new creation. This child stepped out of the normal human procreative cycle. He was human - yet he was God.

The Weapons of Our Warfare

So we begin to understand the precious merits of the blood of Jesus, but how does it become a weapon in our arsenal of warfare?

Beyond the redemptive aspects of the blood of Christ which the writer of Acts calls the purchase price (Acts 20:28), it is the lifeline that keeps us cleansed and "healthy" from the contaminants our enemy would use to weaken our spiritual physique.

First John 1:7-9 spells this out:

> *"But if we walk in the light as He is in the light, we have fellowship with one another and the blood of Jesus Christ His Son cleanses us from all sin. If we say we have no sin, we deceive ourselves and the truth is not in us. If we confess our sins, He is faithful and just to forgive us our sins and to cleanse us from all unrighteousness."*

Not only is the blood of Christ the decontaminant for the individual, it is the life flow of the organism that is the Body of Christ. When we are ingrafted into the Body of Christ at the time of our new birth we become bone of his bone and flesh of his flesh (Ephesians 5:30). Then that circulatory system - the circulating blood of Jesus Christ - cleanses each member of the Body. As we stay in that Body, we continue to receive the life-giving flow of His blood. The Body of Christ is a self-cleansing and a self-healing organism.

Jesus said if we abide in him our barren branches will break forth into productivity. The fruit of the Spirit will start growing because we've been grafted into a cleansing flow that keeps us wholesome and strong.

We stand in awe at the price of our redemption. We can be equally as grateful for the cleansing health produced by the blood of Christ which allows us to become fruitful members of Christ's Body.

But perhaps the most astonishing aspect of the blood of Christ is the protection it affords as a spiritual weapon. Ephesians 6:14 tells us to be sure we have on the breastplate of righteousness. It is the blood of Christ that provides this breastplate.

The righteousness that constitutes our breastplate has nothing to do with our goodness. God clothes us in it as part of the salvation transaction. Paul explains how we get this righteousness in Romans 3:21-26. Since he is explaining this primarily to Jewish believers, I have excerpted it somewhat so that we can pick up its meaning for us.

> *But now the righteousness of God apart from the law is revealed.....even the righteousness of God which is through faith in Jesus Christ to all and on all who believe.....being justified freely by His grace through the redemption that is in Christ Jesus, whom God set forth to be a propitiation (covering)* by His blood *through faith, to demonstrate His righteousness.....that He might be just and the justifier of the one who has faith in Jesus.*

The Weapons of Our Warfare

It is a complete and perfect breastplate that covers the vital, vulnerable organs contained in our breast. Even if a fiery dart shoots by our shield of faith, it will be stopped by the armor of the covering of Jesus' blood and righteousness.

Old-time saints (and modern ones too) constantly would "plead the blood." It comes to their lips readily whenever danger looms. It is a phrase that comforts many a trembling heart. And it isn't a trite cliché. Whether or not they have understood the depths of the covenant, they sing with gusty joy about the power in the blood. Over and over again, they proved, "It worked!"

How do we use this power of the blood in spiritual warfare? How do we attach this breastplate of righteousness to our spiritual beings? In the heat of battle, what can I expect it to do for me. Let's summarize:

(1)) The blood of Jesus initially cleanses me from sin when I become a child of God.

(2)   In my Christian walk, the blood of Jesus keeps me "decontaminated." This is achieved when I confess my sins to Jesus. He is then faithful and just to forgive my sins and to cleanse me from all unrighteousness (I John 1:9).

With the continual cleansing of the blood of Jesus, I am removing those failures and sins that the "Accuser of the Brethren" can use as ammunition against me.

(3) I can enter into rest! The teaching of the fourth chapter of Hebrews assures us that because Jesus as our High Priest has offered the perfect sacrifice for sin - His blood - we can stand still in faith and trust. By taking this seemingly passive

stance, we will wield a powerful blow to the plans of the enemy.

No wonder saints have "plead the blood." You too can wear this protective gear by speaking it aloud when the attacks come. Believe in your heart that the blood of Jesus covers and protects you. Know that in the blood covenant Jesus' sacrifice once and for all has provided protection and covering.

Don't tell me Satan doesn't tremble before the weaponry of the blood of Jesus – the confession of its redemptive power, the pleading of its merits. All hell has to move back when its power is displayed.

It is the answer to all condemnation. It is the mouth-stopper to all the psychological warfare of the enemy. It is the impenetrable covering of the weakest warrior.

> My hope is built on nothing less,
> Than Jesus blood and righteousness,
> I dare not trust the sweetest frame,
> But wholly lean on Jesus name.
> On Christ the solid rock I stand,
> All other ground is sinking sand,
> All other ground is sinking sand.
>
> –Edward Mote

11
The Word of God

And take the helmet of salvation and the sword of the Spirit which is the word of God.

Ephesians 6;17, NKJ

$\mathbf{F}$ew Christians alive have not had teaching on the difference between logos and rhema. It is important to the discussion of spiritual warfare to make some definition. In a sense, it is rhema that turns logos into a spiritual weapon.

As a point of review, logos is the Greek term applied to what we may describe as the written Word. The Bible is logos. The Messiah, Jesus was Logos - the Word become flesh, the the Living Word, the outspeaking of God.

Rhema is logos quickened specifically to an individual.

It is a personalized application to one's heart of logos, the written word.

Another way of illustrating the difference would be to use the symbol of the sword as Paul does. Logos is the sword resting in the scabbard. As we study the word and allow it to dwell in us richly, when we come into confrontation with the enemy, the sword is taken out of the scabbard and brandished. It then becomes rhema.

It is interesting to note that the Word of God is the only offensive weapon listed in the arsenal of Ephesians. All the armor issued - girding or belt, breastplate, foot covering, shield, helmet - is defensive equipment except this sword. So whether it is fastened securely in the scabbard of one's heart or waved in defiance at the enemy, it is crucial that it be kept razor sharp.

We need to commit Scripture to memory letting the Word of God dwell richly in us (Colossians 3:16). We must discipline ourselves to implant the logos into our hearts. It becomes a fund of knowledge filed away in our spirits.

In the verse with which we begin this chapter, rhema is the word used to describe the sword of the Spirit. In order for logos to become a weapon, it must be unsheathed by being spoken.

By speaking the word of God - unsheathing the sword - faith is activated. In Romans 10:17, Paul affirms: "So then faith cometh by hearing and hearing by the word (rhema) of God."

Mark 11:23 tells us that speaking faith can perform the impossible:

The Word of God

*For assuredly, I say to you, whoever says to this
mountain, be removed and be cast into the sea, and
does not doubt in his heart, but believes that those
things he says will come to pass, he will have
whatever he says.*

Even the transaction of personal salvation is accomplished
partly through speaking:

*The word is near you, even in your mouth and in
your heart, that is the word of faith which we
preach: that if you confess with your mouth
the Lord Jesus and believe in your heart that
God has raised him from the dead, you will be
saved.*   Rom. 10:8,9

If what I speak accomplishes so much, can you imagine the
tremendous piercing power of speaking *God's* word to
circumstances, to the attack of the enemy? Attractive as a
sword may be as a den wall decoration, the purpose for its
creation was to cut, wound, stab. That's exactly what is
described in Hebrews 4:12:

*For the word of God is living and powerful, and
sharper than any two-edged sword, piercing even
to the division of soul and spirit, and of joints and
marrow, and is a discerner of the thoughts and
intents of the heart.*

The Weapons of Our Warfare

The original premise of Ephesians 6 is that we are not wrestling against people, but against spiritual principalities, powers, and wickedness in high places. How in the world do I wrestle with a principality, a power, a wickedness? They are such nebulous, nefarious opponents.

People who understand warfare and the concept of rhema are people who are all the time *speaking* to things! They don't keep the Word confined to their hearts, they wield the Sword by giving the Word voice. They verbalize the Word of God. They take the Word out. They wave it!

"Satan, you have no authority. I take authority over YOU, for it is written that sin shall not have dominion over me. I am more than a conqueror through Jesus Christ who loved me and gave Himself for me. Thanks be unto God who always gives ME the victory."

Jesus demonstrated the use of this weapon in his confrontation with Satan as described in Matthew 4. What kind of confrontation was it? It was a verbal duel! Satan himself was quoting Scripture right and left. And as we will see that tactic of his hasn't changed.

The first thing Satan attacked was the deity of Jesus –His identity. "If you are the Son of God, command that these stones become bread."

Jesus answered, "IT IS WRITTEN, 'Man shall not live by bread alone, but by every word that proceeds from the mouth of God.' "

That is the way he comes at us, too. Suppose I proclaim: "I, Coleman Phillips, am a son of God. I'm God's child. I have his authority."

Then Satan will taunt with self-doubts. "What do you mean you're a child of God," he sneers. "Here you are out in the wilderness starving, and you don't even have enough faith to come up with a piece of bread. If God thinks so much of you, why is He letting you stay out here and rot?"

By implanting this thought Satan has challenged my identity, my relationship to God. On the surface it may look like he is saying true things, but when I brandish my sword, I cut to the truth of my relationship with my Father and there is much more involved than whether or not I obtain a piece of bread.

"Do something spectacular, Jesus," was his second challenge. "Throw yourself off the pinnacle of the Temple to prove you've got all this power!"

Jesus said to him, "IT IS WRITTEN again, 'You shall not tempt the Lord your God.'"

He tries the same thrust with me. "Some Christian you are. You'll never do anything great in the Kingdom of God. You blow it all the time. If you really are such a big authority person, prove it. Do something spectacular!"

What he is trying to do is make me cower in fear so I won't come after him. If I look at my own record, I am intimidated, but when I take out the Sword, I understand that I can do all things through Christ who strengthens me. In my weakness, I am made strong in the Lord, and in reality, it is the Lord God he is tempting or challenging.

One can hardly comprehend the brazen gall of Satan in his

third round with Jesus. "All these things I will give you, if you will fall down and worship me." Bribing God to get Him to worship His arch-foe!

Then Jesus said to him, "Away with you, Satan! For IT IS WRITTEN, 'You shall worship the Lord your God, and Him only shall you serve.'"

If conflict won't work, Satan is not at all embarrassed to try to buy us off. He knows our soft spots, and he's expert at hitting our vulnerable areas.

This is why one woman was so perplexed about her circumstances. "Before we were Christians, we had a house that was paid for, two new cars and money in the bank," she complained to me. "Now that we're following the Lord, it seems we have nothing. The bottom has dropped out."

What she had not comprehended was the eternal value system of the Kingdom of God. She had not allowed the Sword of the Spirit to cut her loose from the bondages of the old life.

Satan will use any enticement he can to get you to bow before him. Thousands of Christians are so busy caring for and pursuing their possessions that they never give a thought to the fact that those possessions may be a trick of the enemy to keep them in bondage as much as alcohol, drugs, sex, or any other vice is. Certainly, they are kept too busy to pursue the enemy in spiritual warfare.

Jesus never allowed Satan the opportunity of an argument for if Satan can get you into an argument, he has brought you to his ground. That was the way he defeated Eve. He got her into a discussion about what God had said and what He had meant, and the first thing you know, he had her doubting the goodness of God.

The Bible is not a classic piece of weaponry to be observed. It is a basic issue weapon to be plunged into the vitals of Satan and his henchmen.

That is exactly how Jesus used it. He ignored Satan's insinuations. Every time Satan opened his mouth, he slashed back at him with the Word of God: "IT IS WRITTEN."

With the third and last thrust, He had Satan staggering on the ropes, and I am quite sure He shouted as He demanded, "Away with you, Satan!"

How eloquent the next words: "Then the devil left him, and behold, angels came and ministered to Him."

You don't have to stand around and explain the Word of God to the devil! He knows much better than you what it means. As a matter of fact, he has more faith in the Word than some Christians. He believes it - and trembles! Here is the scenario he likes to engage you in:

"That's an interesting sword you have there. Do you really think it's made of tempered steel?"

"Well, I think so. At least that's what the supplier said."

"You probably paid a lot for it. If I were you, I would be very careful not to break it."

"Well, yes. Maybe I should only bring it out for special occasions."

"And you know, it is a dangerous object to have lying around. Why don't you hang it up on the wall where everyone can admire it, and no one will be hurt."

"That sounds like a good idea. I'll do just that."

That conversation does seem silly, but there's a volume of truth in it. When we lose sight of the fact that the Sword is a weapon, it becomes little more than a relic in our museum of faith.

The enemy will stand around with you all day and quote Scripture. He will admire it with you - anything, as long as he can detract you from coming after him with it.

I strongly believe that people need to study the depths of the Word of God. Those who delve into the history, the languages, the grammar, the contexts, the doctrines, the theologies of the Bible are engaged in worthwhile pursuits. But they need to go beyond the apologetics, the argumentation, even the study of the Bible.

If we are going to counterattack those dark principalities, we must SPEAK to them! We must declare the Word. Shout it. Say to those mountains of doubt or fear, "Move into the sea!" As we speak the Word of God to situations, circumstances, locations, and the assorted hordes of hell, they've got to go. As we stand brandishing our Sword the devil has to flee. The authority of hell cannot prevail.

Both as a person and as a pastor, I've seen victories in battles that were never fought. What do I mean? Let me give you two examples.

As I mentioned previously, I had a physical collapse that altered the course of my life. The weakness and depression held on for months and the depression gave birth to multiple fears. I developed agora phobia, the fear of crowds or enclosed places. Can you imagine how difficult it would be for a pastor to be afraid of crowds? While many portions of Scripture sustained me, one became my sharp sword.

I will bless the Lord at all times, His praise shall continually be in my mouth. My soul shall make its boast in the Lord; the humble shall hear of it and be glad. Oh magnify the Lord with me, and let us exalt his name together. I sought the Lord, and He heard me, and delivered me from all my fears.

Psalms 34:1-4

For months, I spoke and sang this Scripture. And then I would parry with these words: "Satan, in spite of my weakness and fear, in spite of the depression I cannot shake, in spite of everything I feel, I will bless and praise the Lord. And He will hear me, and He will deliver me from my fears."

And one day Satan gave up! He didn't make an announcement. I merely was able to get into my car and drive it and I've been driving ever since. True, I've gone through some stressful times, but I have not had one single day filled with the "blues." The joy of the Lord has become my daily strength.

Every church has its agitators, its whisperers, its backbiters, its strife-makers. Interestingly, these are VERBAL trouble-makers. Of course, the devil gets so excited when he sees he's getting a toehold with some of the congregation that he adds too much fuel to the fire, and the pastor gets a whiff of the smoke.

As pastor, I have the option of going after the trouble-makers, and sometimes to maintain scriptural discipline, I have to deal with them. But many more times than not, Mary and I join hands and come against the Chief Agitator himself.

"Satan," we speak, "no weapon that is formed against us is going to prosper. Every tongue that rises against us in judgment, we condemn right now, in the name of Jesus and on the authority of His immutable Word. Our righteousness is from God himself, and it is our heritage as servants of the Lord (Isa. 54:17). You stop causing those people to sin with their tongues right now.

"We cover any wound Satan has caused in this Body with the cleansing flow of Jesus' blood. We speak healing and wholeness to everyone in our congregation. If there are those, who cannot or will not be healed, Lord, we ask you to remove them so that others will not be weakened. In the name of Jesus, we pray."

By speaking the Word, waving the Sword, we have sent Satan away and released the angels of the Lord to minister to God's people.

If we allow ourselves to get involved in verbal conflict with people, we are playing into the enemy's hand; but when we go to the root of the trouble and cut it off with the Sword of the Spirit, it's amazing how little damage results.

We routinely walk through the rooms of our church facility and speak, "Satan you don't have any authority in this place.

The Word of God

In the name of Jesus, take your troops and get out of here." We lay hands on the seats, we touch the walls, we walk up and down the aisles. We do a lot of speaking and talking that no other mortal hears.

I try to be faithful and diligent in the preparation of the Word of God that I preach from the pulpit, but I can tell you that even though I preached helpful sermons for years, it was not until I learned the secret of unsheathing the sword in private warfare against the enemy who kept my church members bound and sinners at a distance, that I began to see results that could be measured by numerical standards.

"Lord, we lift up the hands that hang down. We speak deliverance. We speak victory. We speak revival. We speak in the name of Jesus that there will be a breaking through of the power of the Holy Spirit throughout the world!"

12
The Name of Jesus

Wherefore God has also highly exalted him and given him a name which is above every name that at the name of Jesus every knee should bow – things in heaven and things in earth, and things under the earth. **Philippians 2:9**

There are two truths that we need to understand when we begin to study the name of Jesus as a spiritual weapon.

First, as believers we have been given the power of attorney for His name. I have discussed this idea at some length in Chapter 9. We have been delegated the authority and prerogatives of the name of Jesus. Although there may be some limitations as to how far-reaching beyond this earth our authority extends, the above Scripture assures us that there are no limits in the universe to His preeminence.

The Weapons of Our Warfare

Secondly, the Name of Jesus is the source of our authority, and our faith is the connecting link that ties us to the source. We don't need faith as much as we need to put the faith that we have in Jesus to constant use. The name of Jesus gives validity to our exercise of authority. It keeps us from being play soldiers in the spiritual arena.

Let me illustrate this by relating a dream I had about another Christian who held a responsible position of leadership. I couldn't understand why people under his direction were always so ineffectual in accomplishing what needed to be done. Before I went to sleep one night I was laboring in my spirit as how to deal with the situation.

In this dream, I saw him as if I were looking at a photograph. He wore full military uniform including guns and the Sam Brown belt for his ammunition. As I looked at him more closely, not only did I see that he had no badge or insignia, but I noticed that the ammunition for his guns was only blanks.

In no sense was this a condemnation of the brother, but rather the Lord spoke to my heart that a person can have position, and yet not have been given the authority to go with that position.

It has long been an accepted tradition in church denominations to emphasize the authority vested in a position. Yet sometimes there are persons in positions of authority who have the uniform on, but have not been issued real ammunition. They have the trappings of ministry, but have no authority or power from above to go with it.

114

The Name of Jesus

These leaders can be very dangerous to follow if one has the expectation that they will be able to effectively lead troops into combat. In the heat of the battle, their blanks do very little good! Without understanding the power of attorney that comes with the name of Jesus, they may shoot their blanks in the air, but the enemy knows he has nothing to fear.

In the Body of Christ, there must be an affirmation of divine authority given to an individual to fit the position he fills. If you have been called and set apart by God, the authority will come with the calling. Other people will recognize it, and more importantly, the devil will recognize it. The Lord will also equip you with live ammunition and the exact weaponry that is needed to conquer the enemy. You'll hit the target. You'll be victorious. You'll find out that your power of attorney makes way for you.

I have been somewhat concerned with some of the faith messages that seem to make faith in and of itself the source of power and authority.

Faith in and of itself doesn't do anything! Ephesians 2:8 reads:

> *By grace are you saved through faith, and that not of yourself, it is the gift of God - not of works lest any man should boast.*

This passage indicates that grace is the source while faith is the vehicle or channel through which grace passes to us.

It is like a water system. The pipe is essential to get the water to me, but I am not looking to the pipe to satisfy my thirst. It's the water that flows through the pipe that is the thing I need. I will keep that pipe in good repair because I need the water, but the pipe without the water is useless.

The Bible is in and of itself only a communication of reality. It is not the reality itself. Jesus said to the Pharisees, "in the Scriptures you think you have life, but they are that which testify of me" (John 5:39).

Just mouthing words, even though they are Scripture, has no power in and of itself. We can get into bibliolatry when we begin to develop formulas about the Word. We can't punch certain buttons in the Bible and get a prescribed answer.

There is not a formula for faith that can be given out like medicine. Faith cannot be superimposed on someone else by following a certain pattern. If it could be, churches with liturgical forms of prayer and worship would be producing the most powerful people of faith people in the land. The Word of God is not the intrinsic source of power. It is the connector to the source—Jesus Christ. That is principle, and not a formula!

While living in the Los Angeles area as a young man, I often rode street cars. They were heavy vehicles—concrete and iron and steel. Occasionally, you would be riding along and the trolley would come off the electric wire. The motorman would go to the back, roll down the window and guide the trolley until it connected once again with the live line.

We are not like storage batteries in our walk of faith. The only time our faith operates is when, like the trolley, we are connected to a live line - Jesus. Faith must connect to our power source or we are not going any place. Our faith vehicle can be constructed of concrete and iron and steel, but unless it is tied to the powerful name of Jesus it is dead on the track.

Why is this true? Why does our faith only operate when we believe on and pray in the name of Jesus? Certainly, God is not on an ego trip. It is because: (1) We need to be constantly aware that apart from our connection to the authority of His name, we have no authority in ourselves and (2) It takes our faith out of the emotional realm. The power of the Holy Spirit does not need to be worked up by human effort. All we need to do is pull the trolley of faith over to our source, Jesus Christ.

Let's consider now why the Name of Jesus is such a powerful weapon. Remember the "principalities, powers, rulers of darkness, spiritual wickedness" that Paul described as being our enemy in Ephesians 6? If we have read the beginning of Ephesians, this sinister group will not seem so terrifying for we will already know their fate. Paul states it this way:

> *That the God of our Lord Jesus Christ the Father of glory, may give to you the spirit of wisdom and revelation in the knowledge of him, the eyes of your understanding being enlightened; that you may know what is the hope of His calling, what are the riches of the glory of His inheritance in the saints, And what is the exceeding greatness of His*

power toward us who believe, according to the working of His mighty power which He worked in Christ when He raised Him from the dead and seated Him at the right hand in the heavenly places, Far above all principality and power and might and every name that is named, *not only in this age but also in that which is to come. And He put all things under His feet and gave Him to be head over all things to the church, which is His body, the fullness of Him who fills all in all.*

Ephesians 1:17-23

At this very moment, Jesus is positioned at the right hand of the Father. He has transcended all the authority structures of this earth, passed through the galactical atmosphere, and has been established in the heavenlies. Jesus is at the ultimate, pinnacle place of authority in the universe.

James Irwin, the astronaut, has been quoted as saying that when he went to the moon he had a deep spiritual experience. As he left the earth's atmosphere, he said that all sense of oppression left him and his thoughts became clear and peaceful. As he wondered about it, the Lord spoke to him that the reason for the tranquility was that he had left the dominion of Satan. All things have been put "under His feet." God is still allowing the rebellion of Satan and sin to play its course, but His victory has been accomplished. He has assumed the position of authority over every realm of the universe. And he has given that authority to the Church so that we now move in the authority of Jesus' name.

Another interesting phrase is Paul's reference: "not only in this age, but also in that which is to come."

It's amazing how difficult it is for some segments of the church to believe the power of God is operating in "this age." On one hand, we have the liberal school that denies any supernatural activity now or in the past - let alone the future.

On the other hand, there are Bible-believing people who have no trouble accepting and defending the miracles of the Bible. Not only that, but they are excited about what Christ is going to do when he breaks through the heavens. They are awaiting the future with great expectancy. Yet neither does this segment accept the fact that the power of God is for here and now. They feel the day of God's power and authority, the day of the miraculous, either never has been or is in a holding pattern at present. In perhaps the most crucial days the world has ever seen, they view the Church as impotent to do anything other than be faithful and wait for Jesus to return.

Scripture spells out the way for the disciple:

And these signs will follow those who believe: In my name they will cast out demons; they will speak with new tongues; they will take up serpents; and if they drink anything deadly, it will by no means hurt them; they will lay hands on the sick, and they will recover. Mark 16:17-18

119

The Weapons of Our Warfare

The prefacing phrase for each of the phenomenon mentioned here is "in the name of Jesus." It is important to establish the authority of Jesus name in all that we do in ministry. It may sound like a simplistic practice, but it cannot be assumed that using Jesus' name is an incidental expression.

Harald Bredesen, one of the patriarchs of the modern charismatic movement who has prayed for thousands to receive the Baptism of the Holy Spirit, states that whenever he prays for someone to receive this gift, he always establishes the name of Jesus Christ in that prayer.

Praying in the name of Jesus for the miraculous takes our petition out of the subjective realm and puts it into the objective realm of God's authority.

One of the reasons we may not experience more of the miraculous is that we become too introspective. We try to figure out if we have arrived in a place where God can use us, or we wonder if there is something hindering our own progress in holiness. I am not minimizing the need for examining ourselves, but no matter how holy we are, we aren't going to be able to produce one single miracle on our own!

James speaks of the "prayer of faith" (James 5:15). We get exaggerated ideas of what the prayer of faith is. We wait for something tremendous to happen, or for some overwhelming emotional feeling. True, some people have had signs that God is performing a healing or miracle, but that is not the usual expectation. It is not a Scriptural requirement.

The Name of Jesus

The prayer of faith is simply praying in the name of Jesus and expecting that simple act of faith - the prayer in His name –to work! The power is not in us; it is in *that name*.

And you have just as much right and authority to use that name as anyone else. You are just as commissioned to perform these ministries as anyone else in the Kingdom of God.

Not long ago, a large growth appeared in the corner of my left eye. Medical people said it looked like a malignancy and I needed to have it removed. I certainly would have had surgery without any guilt that my faith was weak, but I decided to speak to the thing for a while. Each morning and every evening I put my finger on the growth and spoke, "In the name of Jesus I command this growth to wither and die. In the name of Jesus I curse every abnormal cell." It kept getting bigger, but I had received a confidence in my heart that God was going to heal it. One morning as I shaved, I saw that it was gone.

Healing is bread on the table and not pheasant under glass. We get the idea that these signs are the exotica of the spiritual realm. No, they are not; they are the signs that follow *believers*. My believing has nothing to do with my worthiness. It is simply my power of attorney. It is my connection to the source.

When I end my prayer with Jesus' name, the Source yields the miracle. When you begin to move in the simplicity of this truth, you'll be amazed at the miracles that take place. Don't fall into the trap then of cluttering up God's work with all sorts of complications devised by vain and unbelieving men.

The Weapons of Our Warfare

When I was in high school, I wanted to get a job at Universal Studios. Well, I couldn't even get through the front gate. Every time I tried, a police officer turned me away. I tried to telephone for an appointment, but no one would talk to me.

At the time, I was attending school and delivering newspapers with the son of one of the great producers in Hollywood. I told him about wanting to work at Universal. He asked me who I wanted to see. By this time I knew exactly who I wanted to see, and I gave him the name.

In a few days, my friend picked me up in his car (a deluxe Lincoln Continental convertible). We pulled up to the Universal gate, and without a second look, the same policeman who had kept me out so often, motioned for us to drive in. It was the best feeling imaginable to be ushered in because I was with someone who had powerful connections.

That's what Jesus has done for us. Satan keeps telling us, "You can't get in. You have no right to the riches of the Kingdom of God. Who are you?" He keeps flagging us away from the gate.

Then along comes Jesus. "Come along with me," he says, And any time you want to help yourself to all that I have, just use My name!"

13
Praying in the Spirit

*Praying always with all prayer and sup-
plication in the Spirit; being watchful to
this end with all perserverance and suppli-
cation for all saints.* Ephesians 6:18

A scholar I admire said that if you would examine this
particular context in its structure, it could easily be
established that verses 10 through 17 of Ephesians 6 focus on
verse 18. His point is that all spiritual warfare eventuallly
moves into the realm of praying in the spirit.

Praying in the Spirit is where the major battles of spiritual
warfare are fought. Putting on the armor, carrying the shield
of faith and Sword of the Spirit must all be preceded and
followed with mighty, prevailing prayer.

The Weapons of Our Warfare

To understand praying in the Spirit, let us review I Cor. 14:14, 15:

> *For if I pray in a tongue, my spirit prays, but my understanding is unfruitful. What is the result then? I will pray with the spirit, and I will also pray with the understanding. I will sing with the spirit and I will also sing with the understanding.*

From these verses, praying in the spirit can be defined as praying in one's prayer language - praying in tongues.

There are those who tend to dismiss praying in tongues as one of the minor, and indeed, optional manifestations of the Holy Spirit. As a spiritual weapon, I view it as having the awesome potential of a nuclear bomb. Because glossolalia is a controversial subject among believers and there are various levels of acceptance of this practice, I would like to give you six reasons why I believe it is a valid experience for today. For those who fear this weapon, I will spend this chapter acquainting you with its operation.

1. *Tongues are the initial manifestation of the baptism in the Holy Spirit, as they were on the day of Pentecost.*

"Wait a minute," you say, "That's a controversial statement."

Then you point out, as a number of charismatics do that speaking in tongues is not the only evidence for the Baptism of the Holy Spirit. One may have prophecy, or a manifestation

124

of healing, a word of knowledge or wisdom, etc. Any one of these phenomena can be an evidence, you say.

This is not a new concept. In Pardington's Theology, he writes that one might speak in tongues at the time of being baptized, but not necessarily. Any of the other gifts might be in evidence.

This sounds logical, but the argument breaks down. If, on the day of Pentecost, God had wanted to indicate to the Church that a diversity of gifts would be evidence of the Baptism of the Holy Spirit, then why did He not give evidence of those other gifts on that day? Why did not one of the apostles pray for the sick, others prophecy, give words of wisdom and knowledge, or perform miracles?

On the Day of Pentecost, the only phenomenon reported was glossolalia. The only evidence of the outpouring of the Holy Spirit on that day was the supernatural speaking in tongues.

Some have said that this view limits God. The truth is that God sets limits for Himself in many areas. There is only *one* name given under heaven whereby we must be saved (Acts 4:12). There is only *one* place where our faith can rest for salvation –the atoning work of Calvary. We can't be saved by generally having faith in God, we can only be saved through faith in his blood (Romans 3:25). There is only *one* experience that places us in Christ, and that is the new birth. It is not just any sort of religious experience. We must be born again (John 3:3).

The Weapons of Our Warfare

It does not seem unreasonable then to believe that the announcement of the outpouring of the Holy Spirit was accomplished by *one* phenomenon - speaking in new tongues.

I believe the classical Pentecostals were right when they said that speaking in tongues was the initial evidence of being baptized with the Holy Spirit. They did not say tongues were the only evidence, but they did emphasize that they were the initial evidence.

On the Day of Pentecost, those who gathered in the Upper Room spoke in known dialects. The theory has been advanced that God gave them languages so they could go out and preach the gospel. It cannot be discounted, however, that a miraculous enablement allowed those 120 people to supernaturally speak those languages.

There are many documented cases where the gift of tongues has been used by missionaries to preach in languages they have not learned. That use, certainly, is not to be ruled out, and as we approach the end of this age, I believe it will become an increasing phenomenon.

In my own experience, I have prayed in languages unknown to me when there were others present who understood the language.

While pastoring in Hillsboro, Oregon, I was standing at the altar praying in my prayer language after one of the services. I was unaware that my prayer was any different than usual.

A woman who had been a missionary to Indonesia for many years came to me. "Pastor," she said, "Did you know you were speaking in a remote Indonesian dialect? I clearly understood every word you said. They were words of great encouragement to me."

At the time, this faithful sister was a widow and had been having severe physical problems. What a blessing it was for her to receive this "personalized" word of comfort through the ministry of the Comforter.

2. *Tongues are a "Private Code" language.*

The problem with limiting the phenomenon of tongues to speaking in known languages is found in I Corinthians 14:2:

> *For he who speaks in a tongue does not speak to men, but to God, for no one understands him; however, in the spirit he speaks mysteries.*

The primary function of the prayer language is not to speak to men. It was not given to go out and preach the Gospel, but to speak to God. No one else can understand it.

Paul states that we are "speaking mysteries." We are praying with our spirits directly to God, and our understanding is bypassed. Whenever I pray in my native or learned language, it cannot be described as praying in the spirit. I understand the words my mind is formulating and my mouth is speaking. It can't work both ways! Either my prayer is with my understanding, or I am praying in the spirit directly to the heart of the Father and bypassing my intellect.

I do not believe the interpretation of Romans 8:26 should be limited to speaking in tongues, but that ability should certainly be included as part of the interpretation:

> *Likewise, the Spirit also helps in our weaknesses.*
> *For we do not know what we should pray for as we*
> *ought, but the Spirit Himself makes intercession*
> *for us with groanings which cannot be uttered.*

My ability to discover by my own understanding what I *really* need is limited. I do not know the deep needs of my own heart. I certainly am not always able to anticipate the needs of my ministry or my congregation!

The Lord invites us to walk past the deficiencies of our own awareness and move into a realm where the Holy Spirit can take over and begin to pray according to the perfect will of God. He searches the caverns of my heart; and then he makes intercession *for me* with the mind of the Spirit according to the will of God.

The person who prays in tongues is able to bypass the flaws of human understanding and circumvent the interference of the enemy. His petition goes unimpeded to the throne of God.

3. *Tongues allows us to engage in creative prayer.*

The research of Dr. Roger W. Sperry into the thought activity of the brain for which he received a Nobel prize has excited me because of its implication for praying in the spirit.

Dr. Sperry was able to isolate the unique functions of the right and left hemispheres of the brain. He determined that problem-solving abilities flow from the left hemisphere. Intellectual functions and language skills also come from the left side. The right hemisphere is the side of the brain that deals with imagination, conceptualization, creative thinking.

In Western cultures, the left side of the brain seems to be highly developed; while in Eastern cultures, where there is more emphasis on contemplative thought, the right side is more developed. In our culture, by far the larger number of people could be termed "left hemisphere" people.

Occasionally a man like Thomas Edison comes along. He is a "right hemisphere" person, a creative thinker. In the right hemisphere he "sees" or conceptualizes a light bulb —something that has never existed.

Edison took the concept of the light bulb from his right side and began to work on it with his intellect. Following the scientific method, he finally moved the idea from a concept to a tangible article.

Now all the left hemisphere people can recognize it and say, "Oh, yes, that's a light bulb." But it was Edison who first created the concept of a light bulb. So developed was the right side of his brain, that it is estimated that as much as 68 percent of all advances of technology in the electronic field today are still rooted in the inventive genius of Edison.

It has been stated that for every 10,000 individuals who earn doctorates in computer science, only one person can move into the creative realm of conceptualizing new areas of use for the computer.

Not long ago, some tests were made at Fuller Seminary by hooking up electric enciphalagraphs to individuals who were speaking in their prayer languages. One of the discoveries was that these persons were not speaking from the left hemisphere –the normal source of language - but the prayer language was flowing from the right side of the brain. In other words, speaking in tongues is not a function of the intellect.

When we were created in the image of God, two characteristics made us most like him - our conceptualization and our verbalization abilities. Conceptualization flows from the right side - verbalization flows from the left side.

This begins to answer some questions as to why the church lost the power of the miraculous that early Christians enjoyed. Their creative faith shook the world. Nothing seemed impossible for them to believe. When the primitive church moved from being creative people of faith and prayer, they turned to the rational, structured forms invented by the pagan intellectuals of Greece and Rome. Aristotelian logic permeated the teaching of the Church and for generations people remained locked in the confines of their own reality.

Spiritual warfare is often guerrilla warfare. I don't know where the enemy is, what his next move will be or how I should prepare myself to battle against him.

When I pray in tongues, I move into creative prayer. As I am alone before the Lord, as I meditate upon Him, I move into a realm that does not yet exist. As my spirit brings into focus new possibilities, I begin to pray beyond my abilities, believe beyond my understanding; and then by faith as I wait upon the Lord, I see impossible things come to pass in my experience.

4. *Tongues keeps my communication lines straight.*

The most important thing in any relationship is communication. Millions of dollars are spent on psychologists, therapy groups, seminars, books, tapes, etc. to teach people how to communicate.

If there are communication problems present, marriages erode, businesses fail, relationships suffer alienation, wars are begun. Communication that is clearly understood by the parties involved is absolutely essential to progress in any arena of life.

Does it not seem logical that our heavenly Father would take this into consideration when He knows how difficult it is for God and man to relate? This is the most intimate caring relationship that can exist, and yet, there are such broad gaps between God and man. He is infinite and we are finite. He is holy and we are sinful. He is powerful and we are weak. We walk by faith, he is omniscient. We see through a glass darkly. He is the alpha and the omega, the beginning and the end.

Having an easy flow of communication with the God of the universe is beset by other complexities. My attempts at prayer are often feeble. I talk to God because I love Him and I want to tell Him of my love but set myself as I will to spend prolonged periods in His presence, I find myself laboring with lists, with requests, with petitions. I feel frustrated when I run out of things to say - often before I have heard His response! As much as I love Him I just don't know what to keep saying.

Then I feel the fresh breeze of the Holy Spirit as I begin

to pray in tongues. My prayer closet becomes a place I long to visit. It is my rendevouz place with my Heavenly Commander - and my Father.

From my innermost being comes a beautiful language - not from the contrivance of my mind, but from the depths of my spirit. It is a flow of life that transcends my humanity and bridges into His deity. I begin to understand things I do not know as God and I perfectly communicate our hearts to one another in the spirit.

Such spiritual communication excells the most sophisticated of earth's satellite networks. No enemy spy can ever break this code. In the heat of the battle, in the most remote place, in the confusion of life, the Divine Helper sees that my messages get through.

5. *Tongues build me up*.

Tongues are my spiritual R & R - rest and recreation. Eight of the nine manifestations of the Spirit listed in I Corinthians 12:8-10 - word of wisdom, word of knowledge, faith, gifts of healing, working of miracles, prophecy, discerning of spirits, interpretation of tongues - are mainly for the benefit of someone else. Tongues and their interpretation also minister to others but tongues alone are given for my profit.

I Corinthians 14:3,4 continues: "For he who prophesies speaks edification and exhortation and comfort to men. He who speaks in a tongue edifies himself, but he who prophesies, edifies the church."

The word edify means to strengthen and build up. It is a sister word to edifice - to build, building, build up or strengthen.

Praying in the Spirit

Jesus said men should never faint, but should always pray (Luke 18:1). The word faint used here has the meaning of "fainting within." How do I strengthen my inner person? How do I keep from caving in, fainting within?

There is great danger that people in full-time ministry will do just that. Pressures grow nearly intolerable. Vacations and days off give rest to the body, but how does one build up the spirit to keep it from fainting?

I have met many people who feel they have experienced all there is to the gift of tongues because they spoke in them when they were baptized in the Spirit. The use of our heavenly language is not a one-shot or occasional phenomenon. Tongues are not to be used as a certificate to a historic experience.

Kathryn Kuhlman said she would never enter into a day of ministry without praying at least one hour in tongues. It was a discipline for her life and ministry. Perhaps such a discipline would be too mechanistic for some, but if we do not continually avail ourselves of the privilege and the opportunity to build ourselves up in the inner man, we are going to faint.

The danger, the terrible danger, is that we miss the whole purpose of God in giving us this language if we have some kind of watered-down understanding of the significance of speaking in tongues. They are to be used in our lives every day. Praying in the spirit is the fresh flow that holds us steady, that makes us strong, that keeps us from caving in, that gives us access to the perfect will of God, that lets us pray with perfect understanding.

I do not pray in tongues as a devotional function because it makes me feel good, although it does do that. I do not pray in tongues because I feel legalistically guilty if I don't clock in and do it. I pray in tongues because when I do I am tearing down the strong-hold of Satan. I am reconnoitering the enemy's camp. I'm getting clear signals from the Commander-in-Chief, and we are hitting the target with every volley.

6. *Tongues are a unifying force in the Body of Christ.*

"Wrong, wrong, wrong!" the detractors say. "They are one of the most divisive elements in the church and in a loving quest for unity, they ought to be cooled!"

In the beginning of my ministry, I was a strong advocate of that position. "Don't offend your brother," I would rationalize. "We want everyone to feel comfortable when they walk in those doors. Let's save the manifestations of the Spirit for private 'believers' gatherings."

I admit there are two verses in I Corinthians 14 that I could ignore only by convincing myself that they were either muddled by the translator or cultural in their significance.

"Everything must be done for edification in the public service," I argued. "Paul wrote, 'If I do not know the meaning of a language, I shall be a foreigner to him who speaks, and he who speaks will be a foreigner to me. Even so you, since you are zealous for spiritual gifts, let it be for the edification of the church that you seek to excel" (I Cor. 14:11-12).

It was the next verse, the thirteenth, that needled me, "Therefore let him who speaks in a tongue pray that he may interpret." Why would the gift of interpretation be given, or needed, or prayed for if messages in tongues were not to be allowed in the public service?

The other scripture that taunted me was I Corinthians 14:22, "Therefore tongues are a sign, not to those who believe but to unbelievers; but prophesying is not for unbelievers, but for those who believe."

What games we play! How we yield to the intimidation of Satan. If a preacher preaches the whole counsel of God, there is going to be something in it to offend everyone. Starting with the cross and the atoning blood of Jesus, you've offended the proud minds of this world.

Ecumenical unity has been worked at for years with very little success. When there is progress, it is always because someone is willing to compromise one of his tenets of belief. The result has been a mishmash of watered-down humanism.

My view is that it would be a tragedy if all churches came together in one giant monolithic organization. We have already seen the evils of this in church history. My observation has been that diversity and multiplicity provide healthy growth.

We know it is the desire of Jesus that we be one, that we walk in unity. His impassioned plea to the Father was: "that they may be one, as You, Father are in Me and I in You; that they also may be one in us, that the world may believe that You sent Me" (John 17:21).

At this point, we need to put spiritual warfare in perspective. I realize one of the dangers inherent with teaching on this subject is that people may develop a spiritual paranoia where they begin to see demons lurking behind every door.

The Weapons of Our Warfare

Let's set it straight - what this warfare is all about. Why has Satan declared war on us and why must we defeat him? Jesus prayed that He wants the world to believe that God sent him to redeem the world. The devil doesn't want people to know this and certainly he does not want them to experience redemption so he has set himself to kill, to steal and to destroy (John 10:10). Jesus has asked us to enlist in His army and overcome Satan. Our goal is always to see that the prayer of Jesus comes true, "that the world may believe that You sent me."

This is the reason that Jesus prayed for our unity and it is this common purpose that unites born-again believers around the world. It is not denominational affiliation, but membership in the Body of Christ. It is not an organization, but an organism. We are bonded together by salvation through the blood of Jesus. We become blood brothers and sisters.

My further conviction is that the Baptism of the Holy Spirit will bond together a multitude of doctrinal elements into the unity of the Spirit if we will allow Him to do so.

At an interdenominational conference which we attended in New Zealand, a brother came to us at tea time and pointed across the lawn to another man. "You see that brother? He and I have almost nothing in common doctrinally other than our mutual belief in salvation through Jesus, and the fact that we have both experienced the Baptism of the Holy Spirit and speak in tongues. But I dearly love my brother, and we have wonderful fellowship together."

On the plane returning from New Zealand, we talked to

another minister who was on his way to Singapore. "We are having a dialogue meeting of all denominations, and we intend to make plans to permeate Red China with the gospel."

In that dialogue group were Roman Catholic and Anglican priests, Methodists, Congregationalists, non-denominational Charismatics and classical Pentecostals. What was the denominator that brought them together? Glossolalia - speaking in tongues.

Social and political historians have long espoused the opinion that the language barriers of the world contribute to much of the strife on our planet. I believe they have spoken one side of truth. In the account of the building of the tower of Babel in Genesis 11, I believe the other side of that truth is presented. The Lord said, "Indeed the people are one and they all have one language; and this is what they begin to do. Now nothing that they propose to do will be withheld from them."

If such power can be displayed by evil people who are united in a common tongue, what are the potentials for God's people who are united in a common tongue?

God brought to a halt the proud aspirations of that pagan people by confusing the languages so they could not understand one another. Could it be possible in these days of ingathering that He will restore to His people a heavenly language that will transcend barriers erected by traditions of men and unify them in the Spirit around the world so that we can tear down the structures of the Kingdom of Satan and build together the habitation of the most High God?

14

Breaking the Yoke Through Fasting

Is this not the fast that I have chosen: To loose the bonds of wickedness, to undo the heavy burdens, to let the oppressed go free, and that you break every yoke?

Isaiah 58:6, NKJ

Fasting is often the knockout punch to the enemy! There is no surer way to drain the last of his strength.

Millions of Christians pray effectually without the use of either of the divine aids of praying in tongues or fasting. Some believers readily fast as part of their intercessory prayer lives, and still do not avail themselves of the ability to pray in the Spirit. Whether one chooses to pray with his understanding or in the Spirit, when spiritual warfare is hot and heavy, powerful reinforcements come with utilization of the fasting weapon.

According to Isaiah, there are practical as well as spiritual things that happen as a result of our willingness to deny our physical desire for food.

In the spiritual realm: bonds of wickedness are loosed; heavy burdens are undone; the oppressed are set free; yokes are broken. Not bad for missing a few meals!

And in the practical realm, we are shaken out of our egocentric lifestyles to become concerned with the social needs of a humanity that is hungry, poor, homeless, without adequate clothing or protection from the figurative ravages of life. We Christians can so easily become elitist in our smug circles of answered prayer that we forget it's our "own flesh" that is out there broken and bleeding, in dire need not only of saving grace but tender loving care.

Various explanation have been put forth as reasons believers do not engage in more fasting. In affluent cultures, abundance is blamed; among the underprivileged, lack is the cause. As with all spiritual practices, fasting depends on individual response.

My own explanation is that the Church has had the erroneous perception that in order to be effective, all fasting must be grueling. True, there are times when the Lord will call one to fast a number of days. During these prolonged periods, however, there always seems to be an extra grace that rests upon the believer.

In my view, this misperception has caused us to give up the habit of fasting. A common fast in Israel was from sunup to sundown. Often the fast encompassed two such periods or days.

A fast that we have found to be effective and in keeping with our way of life has been to fast two meals for two days of the week. Quite often our church has united to fast for one day in mutual conquest of some enemy.

This corresponds to the so-called Wesleyan fast. John Wesley bound himself in agreement with one hundred Methodist ministers and scores of others to fast two meals on each Wednesday and Friday. It is said that such prayer and fasting kept the Wesleyan revival fires burning for thirty-six years.

There are times when God calls individuals and congregations to special times of fasting, but as surely as prayer is a way of life for the spiritual warrior, fasting should become a regular means for sharpening spiritual senses. The effectiveness of fasting, is not honed through occasional extended seasons of deprivation, but is kept razor sharp by frequent intervals of denial.

Fasting expedites our recognition and successful petitioning before the Lord.

> *But you, when you fast, anoint your head and wash your face, so that you do not appear to men to be fasting, but to your Father who is in the secret place; and your Father who sees in secret will reward you openly.* Matthew 6:17–18

This statement assumes fasting is a routine part of our prayer life.

141

The Weapons of Our Warfare

Fasting is a form of humiliation of the self-life. Not only is it a denial of physical appetites, but it is a part of the process that David describes as a humbling of the soul.

> *I humbled my soul with fasting, and my prayer returned into my own bosom.*   Psalm 35:13

There is no doubt that humility before the Lord is a requisite posture for prayer to be answered. James spells it out in the fourth chapter of his epistle: "'God resists the proud, but gives grace to the humble.' ...Humble yourselves in the sight of the Lord, and He will lift you up" (verses 6, 10).

Fasting puts the impossible into the realm of the possible. In fact, some prayers of deliverance must have fasting as their accompaniment.

> *Then the disciples came to Jesus privately and said, "Why could we not cast him out?" So Jesus said to them, "Because of your unbelief...However, this kind does not go out except by prayer and fasting."*   Matthew 17:19-21

Above all, fasting begins to break our hearts with the agonies that break the heart of God. We can pray with a heart of compassion and, from the prayer, arise to fight the fight of faith that will preach good tidings to the poor, heal the brokenhearted, liberate captives, and open prison doors to those who are bound (see Isaiah 61:1)

Breaking the Yoke Through Fasting

Warfare requires a discipline beyond the average spiritual commitment. Fasting demands that body, soul, and spirit become submitted and committed to the battle. David records the results of such discipline when under attack by his enemies: "When I wept and humbled myself with fasting, I was jeered at and humiliated" (Psalm 69:10, Amplified).

If becomes a matter of priorities. For the duration of the battle, eating well is not an important consideration. If you mention K-rations to a war veteran, he'll grimace. Fighting men can carry only so much weight, and since ammunition is more important than nourishment, the military has developed packets of dehydrated, concentrated food that weigh little and can be kept indefinitely. K-rations are not designed to please the palate.

In Western cultures, food has become a social preoccupation. Jesus, on the other hand, taught us simply to ask Him for daily bread, a necessity of life. A healthy discipline for the spiritual warrior comes when he releases himself from the weights that accumulate in the routine of life. Fasting becomes a spiritual bivouac where all his support systems and resources are stripped to the essential.

The Scriptures concerning fasting have told us that God Himself expresses unique solicitude toward those "special forces" who forgo the pleasures of food in order to humble even their physical bodies before Him. It is an act of total commitment to the fray.

15
Praise and Worship

But at midnight Paul and Silas were pray-
ing and singing hymns to God, and the
prisoners were listening to them. Sud-
denly there was a great earthquake, so that
the foundations of the prison were shaken;
and immediately all the doors were opened
and everyone's chains were loosed.

Acts 16:25-26

As we have previously discussed, the nature of our warfare against Satan is verbal. We unsheath the sword of the Spirit, the Word of God, by *speaking* the Scriptures. As we have discussed in Chapter 14, praying in the spirit or in tongues is a weapon that functions orally.

Praise is another verbal weapon. There are many aspects to

praise. However it is offered, it involves an expressive articulation.

Worship and praise are important to the Lord because they indicate that a voluntary choice has been made on our part. God has designed all creatures to praise and worship Him, but some have chosen not to.

The issue of praise is what started all the trouble in the universe. Lucifer who it seems directed the praise to God (Ezekiel 28) decided that he would exalt his throne above the throne of God and direct praise to himself. The Bible says one third of the angelic host chose to follow Satan and give him their allegiance (Rev. 12:4).

Ever since, all spiritual existence really comes down to the question, "Whom do we worship?"

Second Thessalonians 2 states that during the time of the great tribulation when the abomination of desolation is set up in the restored temple in Jerusalem, the issue will still be worship. The Antichrist will demand worship as he sits in the Temple of God as God.

Our worship, as we are reminded in John 4, is sought by the Father. He seeks those who will worship Him in spirit and truth. The primary reason we were called of the Lord, saved by his grace, is that we might become worshipers.

Worship is the only thing our heavenly Father gets out of all the heartache and tragedy of sin and rebellion. The redeemed people - by choice - volunteer to praise Him. This whole probationary period of sin reigning in the world is allowed, I believe, to test the wills of men. It allows them a choice. That is the sobriety and the dignity of mankind. We can choose to worship God, or we can choose to reject him.

If we do choose to worship Him, an intriguing statement is made in Psalms 22:3. I especially like the New Jerusalem translation: "Yet, Holy One, you make your home in the praises of Israel."

One does not need the fullness of the Holy Spirit to praise God. In the New Testament, believers were praising God even before Pentecost (Luke 24:49). Praise is the deepening of a relationship with God, and with that comes a conscious sense of His blessing upon one's life. It places believers on the doorstep of a new dimension of spiritual life.

Sometimes believers have to praise God as a sacrifice, but there is a great blessing attached to praising God at any time. The sweetness of the presence of the Lord, the sense of the Holy Spirit moving in our lives is so increased when we praise God that it gives high motivation to praise Him continually.

Wonderful as the benefits from praising God are, it is very intimidating to some people. I can't tell you how often people have said to me, "If you would just cool praise in the public service, your church would be four (or eight or ten) times larger."

I've received anonymous letters saying, "I don't want to bring people to your church because of the times of praise. We don't feel comfortable with it."

I well remember the day I first chose to lift my hands in the sanctuary with other believers. I thought everyone in the place was staring at me. My hands felt like lead weights that could not rise higher than my waist.

Praise requires a humbling of the flesh, becoming as a little child - and that's a tough job for anyone's proud flesh.

Hebrews 9:12 states that the blood of Jesus Christ shed on Calvary literally fulfilled all of the blood sacrifices of the Old Testament. When Jesus died, all blood sacrifices ceased. Even Orthodox Judaism does not offer blood sacrifice. The Bible says that Israel would be without an ephod and without a sacrifice (Hosea 3:4). That is true to this day.

The priesthood also changed. The Levitical priesthood was phased out and a new priesthood was established. The born-again Christian now becomes a priest, and every believer is fitted into the Temple of God for a habitation of the Holy Spirit.

Although blood sacrifices are no longer offered, there is a sacrifice that is to be offered by the New Testament priesthood –the sacrifice of praise.

> *By him therefore, let us offer the sacrifice of praise to God continually, that is, the fruit of our lips giving thanks to his name.* Hebrews 13:15

When the priesthood comes together now, we are to offer praise as our sacrifice. While it is primarily a verbal function, there are other ways one can praise the Lord.

Psalms 150 says we can praise the Lord on the trumpet, the timbral, the high sounding symbals, on the drums - there are many musical ways to praise the Lord. We can also praise Him in dance (Ps. 149:3).

However we do it, we are offering back to Him our love and thanksgiving and this is pleasing to our heavenly Father.

When I attended an Episcopal church as a child, my mother taught me that I must be very quiet to show reverence for the house of God. I always equated reverence with silence. Many Christians still do. There is no doubt that contemplation of our holy God can leave us speechless with awe and wonder, but the Bible also teaches that true worshipers make joyful *sounds* (Psalms 89:15)!

In both the Hebrew and Greek, the word for reverence has its root in the word for obedience. When one is reverent before God, one is obedient.

This often requires a yielding of our pride and sophistication. In obedience, we will become like little children who are unashamed to offer a sacrifice of praise, who willingly lift hands in the congregation of the righteous, who lift their hearts with their hands, who lift their spirits and beings in adoration to Almighty God.

> *You also as living stones are built up a spiritual*
> *house, an holy priesthood to offer up spiritual*
> *sacrifices acceptable to God by Jesus Christ.*
> I Peter 2:5

The Christian who remains mute, who does not open his mouth in praise, is going against the direction that the priesthood is to follow in the New Covenant sense.

First Peter 2:9 continues:

You are a chosen generation, a royal priesthood, an holy nation, a people of his own that you should show forth the praises of him who has called you out of darkness into his marvelous light.

Not only is praise of God an act of obedience that the enemy hates, but because praise indicates that we are ones who have left darkness and come into "his marvelous light," it becomes a banner unfurled in the face of the enemy.

There are some incredible records of victories won through praise in the Scripture. The text that we have used at the beginning of this chapter is taken from one of those accounts. Another is recorded in 2 Chronicles.

Jehoshaphat, the King of Judah, was typical of many believers today who waver in their commitment. His heart was turned toward the Lord, yet there were times when he was tempted to enter into an alliance with the wicked Ahab.

As recorded in Chapter 20, Jehoshaphat is faced with a military crisis. The Kingdom of Judah is threatened by the Ammonites and other enemies of Israel.

When he realized the danger of his situation, Jehoshaphat set himself - and then all of Judah - to fasting. This is a good place to note a strong principle of spiritual warfare: Any advancement made in the things of the Spirit will take place only when people in leadership set the example.

Praise and Worship

As Jehoshaphat humbled himself "in Judah they gathered themselves together....even out of all the cities of Judah they came to seek the Lord."

Jehoshaphat led the prayer, "Oh Lord God of our Fathers, are thou not God in heaven?" He reminded the people, himself - and God - who had the authority. Not the Ammonites, not the forces of darkness, but God.

Jehoshaphat continued: "In thy hand is there not power and might so that none is able to withstand thee? Are thou not our God who did drive out the inhabitants of this land before thy people Israel, and gave it to the seed of Abraham, thy friend, forever? (19:6,7)"

"We legally own this land, Father," he reminds. "You gave us this land. We inherited it from you. We didn't come in here on our own. You told us if we marched in here it was our possession. It doesn't belong to these Ammonites. You have disinherited these Gentiles. We are the seed of Abraham - not them!"

Jehoshaphat not only recognized the authority of God in the matter, but the legal right Israel had to take over the land. We can say the same thing under the New Covenant.

"Satan, you are a usurper. You don't have any right here. You have been defeated. I am the legal heir to the covenant promises of the Lord. He has purchased the victory for me. In the Name of Jesus, you must leave!"

Continuing in verse 10, Jehoshaphat reminds the Lord how both the Lord and the children of Israel have been double-crossed: "Behold the children of Ammon and Moab and

151

The Weapons of Our Warfare

Mount Seir whom thou would not let the children of Israel invade when they came out of the land of Egypt, but they turned from them and destroyed them not, behold, I say, How they reward us!"

It doesn't pay to deal gently with the enemy –especially ours! He will always try to cast us out of our own possessions –those to which the Lord has given us title deed. No matter how long he has to wait, he will eventually try to rob all that is rightfully ours.

In desperation, Jehoshaphat cries, "Lord God will thou not judge them for we have no might against this great company that cometh against us neither know we what to do, but our eyes are upon thee" (20:12).

With Jehoshaphat, we acknowledge we cannot fight or win this battle. There is too great a company against us. God always responds to such a cry for help. It may come from reading the Bible, it may come through revelational knowledge, it may come through a supernatural utterance. However it comes, God will direct his warriors as to how, where, and when the victory will be won.

In this situation the spirit of the Lord came upon Jehazeal, the son of Zechariah, in the midst of the congregation and he declared: "Thus says the word of the Lord unto you, 'Be not afraid by reason of this great multitude for the battle is not yours, but the Lord's. Tomorrow go you down against them...You shall not need to fight in this battle. Set yourselves. Stand still and see the salvation of the Lord.' (20:14)".

Praise and Worship

We are not really told how it all came together, but Bible scholars estimate that the group that was appointed by Jehoshaphat included 2,000 singers, 2,000 praisers, and 2,000 worshippers who wore the robes of the priest. They were told to go forth and sing about the beauty of holiness and to praise God for his mercy.

Could anything be more bizarre to human reasoning? The enemy is armed to the maximum. They are ready to fight —to kill! The Israelites are outnumbered 14 to 1. And they are marching out there - *singing!*

Can you imagine what went through the minds of the Ammonites? They are waiting to ambush, wipe out, eradicate the people of God. What an insult - not even a little knife or arrow among the Israelites. How can one have a decent battle with such a crazy army?

> *And when they began to sing and praise, the Lord*
> *sent an ambush against the children of Ammon,*
> *Moab and Mount Seir.* II Chr. 20:21b

Before it was over the Lord caused such confusion on the part of the enemy that they were fighting and destroying one another. I've seen that happen! The enemy never knows what weapon hit him. He becomes confused and literally ends up destroying his own work.

When the weapon of praise is wielded, it also brings a beautiful reward - the spoils of the enemy - great abundance for every area of life. The story ends by stating that it took

153

the Israelites three days to carry out the booty.

In the story of Paul and Silas in the New Testament, a young girl who was possessed by a spirit had followed them for days through the streets of Philippi announcing that they were servants of the most high God.

The girl was speaking truth, but her spirit was wrong. Finally, Paul stopped and cast the spirit out that had given her this knowledge.

> *And when her masters saw that the hope of their gains was gone, they caught Paul and Silas...and brought them before the magistrates saying, These men, being Jews, do exceedingly trouble our city...They cast them into prison charging the jailor to keep them safely, who having received such a charge, thrust them into the inner prison and made their feet fast in the stocks.*
>
> Acts 16:19

The inner prison was maximum security. Not only was it in the depths of earth but, according to Josephus, the sewer ran through these prison pits. Stocks were not an added security measure, but were intended to be a form of torture. Prisoners' arms and feet were stretched so they would be in the most uncomfortable position possible and then the rough heavy bars were snapped shut.

The cold, the stench, the slime, the agonizing pain would not seem to be a prelude to what happened next!

Praise and Worship

In such a setting, I can see myself praying fervently - for deliverance. I can also hear myself crying out for ease from the pain, or calling upon the Lord to bring swift judgment to my captors. But praying and singing the praises of God as Paul and Silas did? - not likely!

The Greek word humnos does not get full translation if we think of it as singing from Page 31 in our Sunday morning worship service. The definition includes singing spirituals, spiritual singing. It does not seem to stretch the meaning to say they were singing in the spirit such as Paul describes in 1 Corinthians 12.

Down in the filth of that maximum security dungeon. Beaten. Their backs bleeding. Tortured. Paul and Silas began to sing praises. What an unlikely spiritual weapon!

One thing about such an unconventional weapon: when you start using it, other prisoners will sit up and take notice. Somehow it is such a strange sound in a world of death that people begin to listen. As believers begin to flash the weapon of praise, the irrepressibility of the life of Jesus breaks forth even in the most unlikely places.

We once owned a home in the San Fernando Valley that had a miserable driveway. Someone started to build it with concrete. The concrete did not set properly so they tried to cover it with blacktop. Some tough species of grass had endured underneath it all.

I would fill in the cracks and coat the driveway to make it look good, but in a short time, the grass would break through all over the driveway. It was the only driveway I ever had to mow!

The Weapons of Our Warfare

As I was working it over for the hundredth time, the Lord spoke to me. "This is just the way my life and power is. It breaks through everything. Nothing can contain it. It goes through the concrete barriers of this life. It will break through walls. It will break through prisons."

As Paul and Silas continued to praise God in the depths of their dungeon, suddenly the earth began to shake under that Roman bastion. The foundations trembled. The doors flew open and the chains fell from all the prisoners. The jailer was so distraught for fear that his prisoners would escape that he started to take his own life. But God's deliverance is not a destructive force. Paul assured the jailer that all were secure. The next words the jailer spoke were, "What must I do to be saved?"

It is my belief that true revival –the great end–time ingathering that so many have prophecied will take place –will be brought about as the people of God come to understand the explosive impact of the spiritual weapon of praise.

A surface shaking, some kind of little religious excitement that passes as the spiritual fad of the moment is not going to release persons chained in maximum security prison houses.

The kind of earthquake that the praises of God's people produce is off the spiritual Richter scale. And God's people are beginning to realize it. In these days before Jesus returns, in these days of restoration and renewal, foundations are being shaken.

Praying and singing in the Spirit can no longer be dismissed as fanaticism or the peculiarity of a certain socio-economic group of people who live on the wrong side of the tracks, or holy-rollerism, or however it has been characterized in the past.

It is penetrating every denomination, every creed, every nation, every social strata. It's coming from leadership down. Everyone is being affected. Prisons are being shaken and people who have been in chains are being set free.

Praise is like germicidal warfare in the spiritual sense. The vapors of this weapon penetrate the deepest dungeons of experience. As they hear the night songs of praise, the prisoners of this world system are given hope. In the throes of death, they begin to sense life.

16
Binding
and Loosing

"And I also say to you that you are Peter, and on this rock I will build my church and the gates of Hades shall not prevail against it. And I will give you the keys of the kingdom of heaven, and whatever you bind on earth will be bound in heaven and whatever you loose on earth will be loosed in heaven." Matthew 16:18-19

One of the most powerful, one of the most significant weapons issued to the Body of Christ is the ability to bind and loose. I say this without fear of contradiction. The traditional teaching that I received, however, lacked a depth of understanding as to all the Lord was saying in the above verses. I had come to the conclusion that the concept of

159

binding and loosing was restricted to the apostles and the early Church.

Perhaps this would be the time to say that if all supernatural happenings were really restricted to the early Church, as some teaching dictates, there would be little left for contemporary believers.

A lack of faith for the miraculous has deprived thousands of believers from seeing the triumph of the Lord in this area of binding and loosing. In my personal life and in the ministry, I have found it to be the strategic arms system in my spiritual arsenal.

Many believers are cautious, or even skeptical about its use. However, this is not optional equipment for the spiritual warrior and by the end of this chapter I believe you will see that we cannot move into triumphant celebration without using this weapon.

The text that is quoted at the beginning of this chapter came about after Jesus and His disciples had entered the borders of Ceasarea Philippi.

> *He asked, "Who do men say that I, the Son of Man, am?"*
>
> *"Some say that You are John the Baptist, some Elijah, and others Jeremiah or one of the Prophets."*
>
> *He said to them, "But who say you that I am?"*
>
> *Simon Peter answered and said, "You are the Christ, the Son of the Living God!"*
>
> *And Jesus said, "Blessed are you Simon Barjona*

*for flesh and blood have not revealed this unto you, but
My Father who is in heaven. And I also say that you are
Peter, and on this rock I will build My Church....''*

It was then that Jesus promised that this revelation of Him
as Messiah would enable His disciples to build His Church in
such a successful manner that even the gates of hell–the
authority of hell–could not prevail against it.

In the Greek language, there is a genuine play on words in
Jesus' comment to Peter. It is a kind of sanctified sarcasm.
It has to do with the size of the rock.

"Peter, you are a stone," is a literal translation.

It could as easily be translated, "Even though you are a
pebble, upon this rock - this foundation stone , this bedrock -
I will build My church. Peter, even though you are small,
your confession of Me as Messiah places you upon bedrock.
This confession brings you into proximity with the foundation - and I am that foundation - the Christ, the Son of the
Living God."

In Ephesians 2 the apostles and prophets are also
graciously included in this foundation and Jesus Himself is
described as being the Chief Cornerstone.

It is at this point that deviation from truth often takes place.
Cults are faulty in their interpretation of the Person of Jesus
Christ. This is what draws the line between the true believer
and the counterfeit.

Being established on the foundation of Jesus alone is basic
to our ability to move in authority as we wage spiritual
warfare.

The Weapons of Our Warfare

The fourth chapter of 1 John spells this out:

> *Beloved, do not believe every spirit, but test the*
> *spirits, whether they are of God because many*
> *false prophets have gone out into the world. By*
> *this you know the Spirit of God: Every spirit that*
> *confesses that Jesus Christ has come in the flesh*
> *is of God, and every spirit that does not confess*
> *that Jesus Christ has come in the flesh is not of*
> *God..*   I John 4:1-2a

It is imperative that we understand that the manifestation of deity was made *in the flesh*. Jesus was not just the highest created being. He was not an angel. He was *deity* made flesh. He was God come down here to be with us. Every spirit that does not make that confession is of the Antichrist. That "revelational confession" is the test of true orthodoxy.

What has all this to do with binding and loosing?

If what the Lord said to Peter was true - that he did not discover Jesus by his own intellectual pursuit, but that it came by divine revelation - how can anyone be saved?

If we can only know Jesus by revelation, then those who teach that salvation is just an arbitrary election process by which God picks out certain people for the revelation and bypasses others, may be right. What is the meaning here?

Nowhere in Scripture does God ever *command* anyone, anywhere to believe for salvation. Of course, the invitation to believe on the Lord Jesus Christ and be saved is repeatedly offered.

The commandment issued from the Godhead to man is not to believe - but to repent! "Truly these times of ignorance God overlooked, but now commands all men everywhere to repent" (Acts 17:30).

If we don't understand this, we find that man's quest for spiritual truth is purely an intellectual one.

Proud man says, "I can't believe because I have so many unresolved intellectual problems. I'm agnostic because so many questions remain unanswered in my mind. Therefore, it is impossible for me to believe or receive Jesus Christ as Savior."

May I say, "Garbage!"

The problem is not that man cannot see; it is because he will not see. It is a problem of the will - and his will has been commanded to repent.

Peter was astounded when he went to the house of Cornelius and discovered Gentiles praying and giving alms to God when they had not as yet heard about Jesus Christ. The Holy Spirit was dealing with them before Peter arrived. Something had happened in their hearts that caused them to repent.

The Holy Spirit is about the same work in the world today. He is convicting people of sin. He is trying to get us to acknowledge our sinful nature and herein lies the problem.

Arrogant hearts will readily be involved in intellectual, spiritual, religious discussions, but only the withering work of the Holy Spirit can cause them to cry, "I've blown it. I've broken God's law. I am morally bankrupt. Everything else may be going for me, but I'm a sinner. I'm unclean. My lifestyle stinks, and I need to get low before God in repentance."

Why would God entrust the revelation of a Savior to someone who feels no need to be saved? Until someone realizes he is lost, the concept of a Savior is foreign.

I remember well the season of my life when the Holy Spirit began to pierce my smug mind. My grandmother had long prayed for me and occasionally she would try to convince me of my need for Jesus. She wasn't an intellectual; I could always out-argue her. To my high-faluting rebuttals, she would simply reply, "Colie, all I know is you need Jesus Christ. Without Him, you're lost!"

I would wrap my pride around me and give dear, old eccentric Nanny a patronizing hug but late at night, lying on my bed, the Holy Spirit would hammer her words into the depths of my arrogant spirit.

You're unclean. You're life is out of sync. You're a sinner. You're lost. You have no hope. You need to repent!

I didn't have any idea what it all meant. I just knew I had to find the answer - not for my intellect, but for my uncleanness! Whatever the Holy Spirit was saying, whoever and whatever He was, I knew at my very gut-level He was absolutely right about me. I was a sinner. I was convinced of that.

Almost simultaneously the revelation of who Jesus Christ was came to me. I can remember the day; I can remember the hour. I had read John's gospel a hundred times in my church experience, but that time as I read, the words leaped out at me. And my spirit leaped back at them.

"He's alive! He is a real person! He is not just a historical myth, but He is living now. He really died for my sins. His bloodshed meant something - my salvation. And He *loves* me." Oh, yes, I knew beyond a shadow of a doubt that God loved me.

I began to read the Bible, and I read and read and read. I couldn't get enough. Why? Intellectual understanding had not finally dawned on my haughty mind, but God had caused my hurting, sinful heart to come to a place where I just gave up. I gave up the fight to maintain the pride of the flesh, and I humbly spoke the words, "Jesus, I need you. I don't know what You're going to do for me, but please do something."

Repentance for sin and a revelation of the Savior does not generally appeal to the cool sophisticates of this world so the religious system promotes a semblence of orthodoxy that allows people to go around that part. They try to open a more pleasing side door to salvation.

However one perceives his intellectual or social status, it is the ultimate stupidity to build on such a fragile foundation. Unless hope for salvation is firmly founded on the rock of the saving grace of God through Jesus Christ - the same Rock upon which Peter founded His confession of faith - the flood waters of life will sweep it away. At best such religion is a temporary accommodation that has no eternal worth.

Jesus said, "Peter, I'm going to build My church and it will be based upon this rock: confession of Me. Nothing can move the Church while it is based on that confession. Not only that, but I am going to implement the weaponry of My Church with executive privilege. I'm going to give you the keys of the Kingdom. Whatever you bind (prohibit, forbid) on earth shall be bound in heaven. Whatever you loose (permit, let) on earth shall be loosed in heaven."

Traditionally the Church has said this was an apostolic prerogative granted to Peter only. In chapter 18, verse 18, a far more inclusive use is indicated. The promise was made to the total entity of the Church.

When we become Christians, as we have stated previously, we become citizens of the Kingdom of God. Now to these citizens, God is granting certain powers by giving us the keys of that kingdom.

In those times, keys were a symbol of authority. There are several explanations as to what Jesus was alluding in the use of this symbol. I think the one set forth by the International Bible Dictionary is particularly insightful.

Upon completion of rabbinical training, the religious leaders were given long chains to wear about their necks from which hung keys. Three privileges were then theirs:

First, they could open the cabinets that housed the Scriptures. Thus they had access to knowledge.

Secondly, they had the authority to adjudicate, to make judgments between right and wrong.

Thirdly, they had the power to set forth new legislation.

For much the same reasons, we have need for the keys of the

kingdom of God. We are engaged with Satan in a jurisdictional dispute. Jesus invaded this planet and established His domain right under the nose of Satan. And Satan is not going to give up any of his domain without a fight.

Satan will stand at his gate and taunt the Christian, "That loved one is mine. You can't have him. I'm going to tie up your finances and impoverish you. I'm going to bring disease upon you and destroy you. I'm going to keep you in constant turmoil and discredit your testimony. I'm going to rob your peace and steal your joy, and do anything else I can to kill you."

Then he roars, "This is my realm of authority. I've locked you out. You can't have anything that's mine. You're defeated!"

Jesus says exactly the opposite. He says there isn't anything that can prevail against you. There is no area from which Satan can lock you out. You have the keys of the Kingdom!

You have the knowledge to understand the enemy's strategy. You have the title deed signed by the heavenly recorder. You know what belongs to you. You make judgments as to what is legally and rightfully yours. You legislate the lines of jurisdiction. You tell the devil where to go - you don't concede to his terms.

The posture of the Church is not to be cowering in a fearful, defensive position, but to be moving aggressively through Satan's gates, his authority, unlocking every door upon which he has posted "no admittance," and taking back everything that God says is ours.

The Weapons of Our Warfare

Our commander has invested us as the people in authority. We are to rule and reign. That jurisdictional privilege has been given to us. We establish it by binding and loosing –forbidding and prohibiting, or releasing and letting.

In the Greek, the future subjunctive mood is used in the first part, and the last part is written in the perfect tense. It could be translated: "Whatsoever you shall be binding, shall already have been bound. Whatsoever you shall be loosing, shall already have been loosed."

At one point in our ministry, there was a woman in our church who was a notorious trouble maker. People stood in line to tell us to watch out for her when we first took the pastorate. The woman was a compulsive liar, but a very convincing one. The first time we had trouble with her rather than trying to call the people involved and straighten the matter out, Mary and I joined hands and prayed this prayer of agreement: "Father, in Jesus Name we prohibit and forbid anything this woman has said to cause damage to the individuals or to this congregation. Whatever is causing her to behave in this manner we release for your Spirit to heal."

Every time we heard something troublesome about her, we agreed together in the same prayer. A joke between Mary and me used to be that we "bound" that woman so many times, it was a wonder she could get out of bed! Although she did not come to a place of repentance while we knew her, as far as I can recall, she never caused us or the congregation any trouble. Her influence had completely dissipated.

There is a contingency involved in binding and loosing. It

seems apparent that if one does not prohibit or release, then things will go on as usual. In other words, the strong man has already been bound in heaven, but you must take the step of binding him on earth.

We bind and loose by speaking in prayer what we want prohibited or forbidden. For example, when our sons were going through times of temptation in the area of relationships, or habits or spiritual decline, we would specifically name those things. In addition to asking the Father to bind it in heaven, we would tell Satan that we forbade his intrusions into the lives of our children, that we were setting the limits and our household was off-limits to his activity.

Loosing or releasing allows the ministry of the Holy Spirit to move into areas of warfare. On the other hand, we can command Satan to release the bondages he has placed upon people. There are so many people enslaved to addictions and habits. Through the prayer of loosing we can start the process that will give them liberty, set them free to be all that God has designed them to be.

In Matthew 12:26, Jesus gives us further understanding of this weapon:

> *If Satan casts out Satan, he is divided against himself how then will his kingdom stand?.......But if I cast out demons by the spirit of God, surely the kingdom of God is come upon you. Or how else can one enter a strong man's house and plunder his goods, unless he first binds the strong man? And then he will plunder his house.*

The Weapons of Our Warfare

We must develop the faith to understand that the authority we exercise has already been validated in heaven. The strong man has been bound provisionally and potentially by the finished work of Jesus, and we are able to continue plundering his goods and his house by completing the transaction of binding here on earth. From heaven's side of things, it is a finished transaction. The nature of our warfare is not going in and subduing the enemy by fighting and winning the battle. That has already been done by Jesus. The strong man has been bound. We are called to establish the victory by reclaiming the spoils–the lost souls, the relationships, the peace, or whatever!

Another reality of spiritual warfare is that we fight an invisible enemy who has an invisible kingdom and, for the most part an invisible army.

Jesus illustrates this in Matthew 7 with the story of the tares. Tares are counterfeit or bastard wheat or darnel. You can't tell the difference between the genuine grain and the tare until you open it up to discover if there is a kernel inside.

The Lord said an enemy had sown those tares. And they are sown right in the middle of the field - the symbol of the true church. The tares are in such close proximity to the real believer if you start to pull out the counterfeit, you might damage the good grain. Leave it alone, he cautioned, don't touch it. So how do you fight Satan in this situation?

I've seen a lot of bastard wheat in my ministry. People come into the Church who want to divide, to uproot, tear down, destroy - and you can't fight them directly because they always attach themselves to some good wheat. They are motivated by the powers of hell and they operate as a phantom force. They deal in the realm of subtlety, in the realm of innuendo, in the realm of rumor, in the realm of the nebulous. You know its there, but you can't touch it.

What are we to do? Are we to sit around and wait for the enemy to come in and tear our churches apart, ruin the harvest, discredit the work of the Kingdom of God? Don't we have any options? Any alternatives?

Oh, the great relief to have the Lord thrust this weapon of binding and loosing into your hand!

"Coleman," He encourages, "whatever you prohibit, I have already prohibited. Whatever you forbid, I have already forbidden. Go ahead, put the straight jacket on it down there, and you can be sure it's straightjacketed up here in heaven. I'll be right there with you! You're one of my followers in Escondido. I've given you jurisdiction over that area. Make the enemy flee."

17

To Fight or Not to Fight?

(But isn't God Sovereign?)

Pray without ceasing. 1 Thessalonians 5:17, KJV

"**I** couldn't care less about theology," say some. "It is a lot of technical terminology that has little relevance to my practical Christian walk."

If that is one's understanding of theology, he is open to all sorts of deception by the enemy. Whether it is in technical terms or an intuitive conviction, the exposure each of us has had to theological systems and doctrines will profoundly affect not only our spiritual world view, but our resolve to deal with the enemy.

A recent best-selling book has taken many ministries, especially television ministries, to task. The book implies, among other charges, that a few of these ministries border on the cultic. Some of the accusations sound as if they have validity.

As I have listened closely to both the attack and the defense offered by my brothers, my heart has been moved. It seems apparent to me that because the leaders under siege have not come from strong theological traditions, nor have their backgrounds made them aware of the doctrinal issues under consideration, they are vulnerable to criticism. As I have heard their explanations, my impression has been that they do not comprehend the reasons for the attack. That is not to say the attacks do or do not have merit. It is to indicate that Christian brothers are operating at widely diverse levels of understanding.

To say we don't care about theology is analogous to the people of the World War II era who thought the German philosophers were boring academics who should be tolerated bemusedly or totally ignored.

Adoph Hitler did not ignore them. As a teenager he devoured the work of Nietzsche, the philosopher who said, "Might makes right."

That small concept planted as a seed in the mind of a lunatic brought a final reaping of destruction responsible for the death of 43 million human beings, including eight million Jews annihilated by Nazi "might."

Philosophy made its devastating impact on millions of young servicemen who had never heard of Nietzsche, let alone read his arrogant writings.

There is a widely taught theological approach that, stated

simplistically, holds this view: God is so sovereign that everything in the life of a Christian is predetermined. These theologians leave little leeway for the freedom of human will. They go so far as to say that even in salvation, the sinner is a passive participant. In a specific decree of God–determined before the foundation of the world–it was ordained that this person come to the Lord Jesus. That decree finally catches up with the individual, and salvation is the result. There are many shades of this teaching.

Any thinking person, of course, must affirm the sovereignty of God. The issue here is not His sovereignty, but how it is defined in relationship to what He created in His own image and gave dominion to rule over all those things listed in Genesis.

There is something subtle and insidious in the theological approach that ultimately sees man as a pawn to be played by the capricious hand of God. This perception effectively puts one off from moving aggressively into spiritual warfare.

Here is the natural progression of that theological bent:

"Everything is in God's hands, isn't it? Then what is going to happen will happen. Whatever will be will be. I cannot change it."

On the other end of the spectrum, this teaching will often produce bitterness toward God. Rather than Christian passivity, this extreme teaching of sovereignty commonly produces Christian hostility.

"God, why have You allowed this to happen? If You hold all the cards, why didn't You prevent it?"

The Weapons of Our Warfare

In counseling we deal regularly with Christians who are angry with God. In their anguish, they have accused God of instigating the hellish attack that has come their way.

For the first ten years of my ministry, I was bound by good doctrinal intentions, but they were persuasions that put both God and me in such theological confines that I was virtually impotent in ministry.

On one hand, my extreme position on the sovereignty of God approached fatalism. Then, in an effort to let God off the hook so He would not appear to be arbitrary or mean-spirited, I grasped a strong dispensational approach to God's working with humanity. As I explained at the beginning of this book, that view divides God's dealing with man into historic segments. This provided me with the logical reason that God could not do other than what His sovereign decree had etched into the eternal scheme of things for our particular time or dispensation.

I spouted the timeless cliché of faith: "Prayer changes things." But in my heart I believed it did very little good to pray, as God has already predetermined what was to happen.

If prayer meetings are a validation of the motto I have just quoted, ninety percent of the Church joined with me in not believing it! It has been said that prayerlessness is the greatest sin in the Church today. Prayer is the hardest thing to do on a consistent schedule.

I believe this absence of vital, powerful prayer in the Church has much more to do with theology than indifference. It goes back to our concept of God. Filtering through our mindsets is this kind of rationale: "Well, God knows where I am. God knows my needs. God knows what is going on in my life. He knows where I live. When it's God's time, I'll be delivered."

What a devious strategy of the enemy! How it cripples our prayer lives. This teaching of Christian resignation plays right into Satan's hand.

If I believe everything in my life is coming from God, then what motivation–other than for grace to bear the trial–would I have for praying? How discouraging! How frustrating!

The thorn in Paul's flesh is offered in support of the idea that God sends trials the way of the Christian, and one would have to agree that God's purpose was involved in the thorn. But there was an explanation for the thorn, and its origin was identified: The buffeting of Satan was an "allowing" of God for a specific purpose to keep Paul from becoming conceited at the great revelation given him (2 Corinthians 12:7).

If God has told you specifically that He will not remove the thorn from your own flesh, then trust in His mercy and goodness. If God is dealing in a special way, ministering something unique and personal, there will always be an explanation, a whispering, "My grace is sufficient for you."

But be sure you have heard Him speak this to you before you give up the fight against Satan! A permanent "allowing" is the exception; healing and freedom for God's children are the rule.

Don't be confused! God is not our adversary! The devil is our enemy, the force and power against us. It is God's purpose to cause us always to have the victory. It is the enemy's goal to destroy, to steal, and to kill.

A spiritual warrior's understanding needs to encompass the "nows" of God's timing. God has already moved. He has already won the battle. He has already made provision for us to live as victors and not victims.

It is as though he has said, "I leave a latitude of freedom with you. What you do with it is really going to make a difference. If you don't pray, certain things won't happen. If you do, certain things will happen. If you don't fight the good fight of faith, you will live defeated. If you do, you will be more than a conqueror."

In an earlier chapter we talked about the parable of the wheat and the tares as a reason for using the weapon of binding and loosing these entrenched but intangible foes.Once again, for illustrative purposes, I would like to refer to this parable.

We once attended a church where we could actually observe the encroachment of the tares upon the good grain. The identification of the tares became less and less difficult. All one had to do was observe the devastating influence they had on the people with whom they associated.

What had been a flourishing church filled with love and purpose became a Body torn with strife. The pastor tried to deal with the mounting discontent by placating the tares. When that no longer worked, a business meeting finally brought into confrontation all factions, and with one searing blast from the enemy's torch, ripe wheat as well as young shoots were forever scorched.

It wasn't the first, nor the last, time I have observed the